HEATH LEDGER

HOLLYWOOD'S DARK STAR

HEATH LEDGER

HOLLYWOOD'S DARK STAR

Brian J. Robb

Plexus, London

CONTENTS

INTRODUCTION

'People always feel compelled to sum you up,
to presume that they have you and can describe you.
That's fine. But there are many stories inside of me and
a lot I want to achieve outside of one flat note.'
– Heath Ledger

On the afternoon of 22 January 2008, in a vast SoHo apartment in New York City, the light of a rising star flickered and failed.

Heath Ledger, only 28-years-old, had long since earned an unusual dual status as both movie heartthrob and serious thespian. He'd reached a fork in his career rare for one who had originated so far outside the Hollywood firmament, when he could have chosen the route to either international superstardom or complete mastery of his craft. Maybe even both.

There was no doubt among those who witnessed his recent work that the path less-trodden beckoned. With an increasing number of risk-taking, bravura performances to his name, Ledger seemed on the cusp of elevating himself well beyond the 1990s generation of 'Hollywood hotties' he had once been associated with – perhaps becoming the stuff of screen legend.

But fate would decree that, though Heath Ledger would indeed take his place among the Hollywood pantheon, it would not be within his own lifetime.

His was the first unexpected celebrity death of the Internet age, where news travels instantly around the world, feeding a ceaseless 24-hour hunger for information. As a result, during the initial stages of the investigation into the circumstances of his passing, much misinformation was presented as fact, and speculation as to the cause of death and Ledger's lifestyle was rife.

Heath was hailed as various things, from the new Mel Gibson to the new Marlon Brando. He was a poster boy for heroic action movies like *A Knight's Tale* and a thoughtful actor who played minor roles in art-house movies like *Monster's Ball* and *I'm Not There*. Even during his beginnings in the clever – but ultimately

'I always go through the process of hating the role, hating myself, thinking I've fooled them,'
said Heath of the pressures of being a high-profile young actor.

disposable – teen flick *10 Things I Hate About You*, Heath harboured artistic ambitions that Hollywood seemed ultimately unable to fulfil. Despite his teen movie start and lack of formal training, Ledger grew into a serious actor, someone who wanted to be challenged by his craft and to lose himself in his roles.

'I was eighteen-years-old,' he remembered of his start in American movies. 'The idea of being an Australian from Perth and getting offered a movie with Touchstone Pictures? I was like, "Who gives a fuck? Put me in your movie!" I thought, If I don't take this, maybe nothing will ever happen.'

Despite his enthusiasm, Heath was not simply dazzled by the offer of a big part in a studio movie. He knew it would give him his start, maybe even put him on the map, but he had bigger ambitions and he also knew that he could only rely on himself and his own innate talents to realise them. 'It still often feels like a whole load of bullshit,' he admitted of the film industry, 'and just acknowledging that puts me at ease. When I first worked in the industry, it seemed so unbelievably foreign and surreal. The differences between good and bad people were so extreme. The way some people treated others, or held themselves so falsely high, disgusted me, and I promised myself I'd never become like that.'

The young actor quickly took stock of Hollywood and didn't much like what he saw. Hard as it was to resist, Ledger wanted to avoid being sucked into that superficial and profit-driven way of life. 'From 18 to 22, I was alone, living in LA with a bunch of friends, partying. I don't know if I knew, or cared to know, what I was capable of back then. I guess I'm just starting to, for lack of a better word, care more,' he said of his need to move beyond teen roles and into challenging adult parts.

Movie executive Amy Pascal was supervising production of *The Patriot* when she singled Heath out for stardom on a scale he scarcely could've imagined – or wanted. 'You always know when you meet somebody who's going to be a movie star, because they sparkle,' she told *Interview* magazine. 'As much as Heath sometimes tried to hide his sparkle, it just came through. It was that boyish, sexy, misunderstood, James Dean thing that we are always looking for. He had it.'

Heath had been snapped up by über-agency CAA, and was being represented by Steve Alexander. He saw the same potential in the new signing as Amy Pascal. 'When Heath first came into my office, he was seventeen-years-old. He had all the characteristics of a man, and yet he was a boy. But you could just feel that there was something important going on right away. Everyone who met him had that impression of him.'

Amy Pascal was instrumental in giving Heath leading-man status in Brian Hegeland's witty period adventure movie *A Knight's Tale*. Ledger knew that to get on in the movie industry, there would be sometimes undesirable demands made of him, and that this early in his career, he was in no position to turn down a could-be blockbuster in favour of the more modest, serious movies he was really interested in. He did, later in life, consider what might have happened to him if he'd snubbed Pascal and the offer from Columbia. '[I'd] probably [be] in drug rehab, or living a layabout life in Miami,' he speculated. 'I knew I was being offered a deal with the devil. I didn't trust it, it felt short-term, they weren't going to take responsibility for me if I fried. I also felt professionally cheapened – like, "Is that all they think I'm capable of."'

Despite his reservations about the film, and his major problems with the work required of him to promote it, *A Knight's Tale* put Ledger on the movie-star map. Here was a new talent, and big things were expected of him. The tragedy of Ledger's short life is that he didn't always fulfil these expectations, either those others had for him or those he held for himself. Throughout his career, he was featured in a string of box-office or artistic failures, including historical epic *The Four Feathers*, horror thriller *The Order*, and skateboarding movie *Lords of Dogtown*. 'I know there's a master narrative out there that says Heath was in these terrible movies, but I beg to differ,' said *Brokeback Mountain* producer James Schamus.

Actress Naomi Watts was romantically involved with Ledger on-and-off over the course of two years, and she knew that the path mapped out for him by movie executives was not one he wanted to follow. 'At first, people were trying to shape him as this kind of teenage hunk. And that's so not what he wanted. It was something that he was trying to escape into the world of real artistry. When I met him, he was just turning that corner in his work.'

Ledger proactively 'destroyed' his 'manufactured' career, feeling he had to be seen to fail in some big movie before he'd be allowed to go off and do his own thing artistically. It was the only way the young actor could see to escape from the teen idol tag that was attached to him. 'It was like I diverted off the map and took a back road to the place I wanted to get to,' he said, describing his risky route to artistic achievement. 'I'm on a journey. I'm on a walkabout [an Australian Aboriginal coming-of-age ritual]. A lot of people think ambition or success, and they think dollars . . . My success is getting underneath that. At the end of the day, that's the only thing you're going to carry with you when you die.'

On the set of *Ned Kelly* he struck up a relationship with Naomi Watts, and it was her who urged him to accept a role that had been seemingly turned down by every young actor in Hollywood: Ennis Del Mar, the ranch-hand who falls in love with a male rodeo rider in 1960s America. His CAA agent, Steve Alexander, recalled: 'He wanted to take parts that were more complicated and more difficult. He wanted to play characters that he could disappear into and not [be] the leading man, which might have been an easier path for him. I think that started with *Monster's Ball*, and then obviously, when he decided he would take on the part of Ennis Del Mar in *Brokeback Mountain*.'

If ever there was a challenging role, it was this one. 'He feared it,' Alexander said of the intense commitment Ledger would bring to the taciturn part. '[That] is what made him go towards it. I don't know if he understood completely the importance of what he was doing at that moment, but I think he knew that he was doing good work.'

Ang Lee also recognised the latent talent Ledger was beginning to show. 'He had that macho, western, non-verbal, turn-of-the-last-century aura,' said the *Brokeback* director of his leading man. 'He carries both aggression and fear, like two sides of a blade.'

For the first time, Heath threw himself body and soul into playing a role, a habit he was to continue to indulge for the rest of his career, much to his mental and physical detriment.

Untrained as an actor, and with very limited juvenile stage work, Ledger was learning his craft on the job. Part of his desire to seek out roles in unusual films was a need to challenge himself, to make sure that in acting terms, at least, he kept himself fresh. 'I don't have a technique,' Heath claimed of his approach to movies. 'I've never been a believer in having one set technique on how to act. There are no rules and there is no rulebook. At the end of the day, it all comes down to my instincts. That's the one thing that guides me through every decision professionally. That's my technique. You read through the script 100 times. I guess I have little characteristics about myself. Sometimes, most often than not, once we start shooting I won't look at the script at all until we finished shooting. It's kind of like it's been imprinted in my head during rehearsals. You just let it go.'

Letting go didn't come easily to Heath. Starting with *Brokeback Mountain*, he deliberately immersed himself in each character he played, absorbing something of them into his very personality. For most roles, like Ennis, or Casanova, this didn't present too much of a problem. But for an uncompromisingly dark characterisation like that of the Joker in Christopher Nolan's *Batman Begins* sequel *The Dark Knight*, the implications for Heath's mental health were a little more serious. 'I'm always gonna pull myself apart and dissect it,' said Ledger of his on-screen work. 'I mean, there's no such thing as perfection in what we do. Pornos are more perfect than we are, because they're actually fucking.'

Heath often felt something of a fraud, as if he'd fallen into acting by mistake and would be found out at any moment. 'I always go through the process of hating it [the role], hating myself, thinking I've fooled them, I can't actually do this.' Even his Oscar nomination for *Brokeback Mountain* did not put Heath's mind at rest about his own talents. 'I've never been in a movie that people liked so much, so I'm really suspicious of it,' he said of the unanimous critical success. In fact, his success only added to his stress. An unnamed English film director told *New York* magazine: 'He was in a terribly anxious state during the Oscars. The day after the Oscars, he said to me, "I'll never make another good film again." If this was what happened when you made a good film, he didn't think it was worth it. He found the whole thing absolutely harrowing. I think that after the Oscars, there was a kind of corner turned – and not a very good one.'

Heath was a big sufferer of performance anxiety when it came to his screen craft, and it was something he always had to overcome. 'Performance comes from absolutely believing what you're doing. You convince yourself, and believe in the story with all your heart. I believe in my performance. And if you can understand that the power of belief is one of the great tools of our time and that a lot of acting comes from it, you can do anything. Your personal evolution runs hand in hand with your professional evolution. Performance and the person you are kind of grow simultaneously.' Occasionally, though, Heath's belief in his own performances would falter, causing him worry well beyond the call of duty.

Heath took a risk by rejecting the teen idol career path that had been laid out for him, and ultimately reinvented himself as an A-list Oscar nominee.

On finishing *Brokeback*, and feeling stressed out at the demands the part had made on him, Ledger immediately flew to Venice to start work on the light-hearted period romp *Casanova*. However, his return to Australia to shoot harrowing drug addiction drama *Candy* brought the actor a new series of challenges. In preparing for the part, Ledger researched with real-life drug addicts and convincingly denied he'd had any experience of drugs himself, beyond smoking pot. After his death, allegations of a hard-partying, drug-dependent lifestyle emerged, revealing a new aspect of his character.

Heath Ledger's final months were fraught and difficult. Over the years he'd enjoyed a variety of high-profile relationships, often with other actresses or co-stars significantly older than he was. His initial romance was with his TV co-star Lisa Zane, who helped bring him to the US. A dalliance with Australian model Christina Cauchi was an on-off affair, but he had other relationships in between reunions with Cauchi, such as those with actresses Heather Graham and Naomi Watts. Finally, Heath settled down with actress (and *Brokeback Mountain* co-star) Michelle Williams, two years his junior, and they had a daughter, Matilda, who was two-years-old when he died. In the fall of 2007, Ledger and Williams split up, causing Heath untold anguish. He'd thrown himself deeply into his work that year, playing the role of the Joker in *The Dark Knight*. 'I want it to be a very sinister kind of thing,' Heath said of his Joker. 'I definitely have something up my sleeve. I just instantly had an idea of how to do it.'

Ledger's immersion in the mind of the psychopathic Joker, combined with ongoing harassment from the paparazzi (which he had suffered more intensively than ever since *Brokeback Mountain*, especially in Australia), his anxiety and continued inability to relax or sleep, plus his worries about his future relationship with his daughter, troubled the actor deeply. Indeed, it seems that no one knew quite how deeply until it was too late. 'He had uncontrollable energy,' said Michelle Williams. 'He buzzed. He would jump out of bed. For as long as I'd known him, he'd had bouts with insomnia. He just had too much energy. His mind was turning, turning, turning – always turning.'

Heath Ledger's reliance on prescription medicines was growing, and it was this that would lead to his unexpected and tragic death on 22 January 2008, during the shooting of his final film, Terry Gilliam's *The Imaginarium of Doctor Parnassus*. The worldwide outpouring of shock and grief that followed showed what an impact the young actor had made on audiences and the Hollywood movie business. At only 28-years-old, Heath Ledger was gone, at a time when it was clear he had so much more to give. His life was short, but he'd packed a lot of living in.

'A lot of people think ambition or success, and they think dollars,'
Heath said. 'My success is getting underneath that.'

1. STARTING OUT

'My parents left my soul and spirit untouched.
They gave me nothing but confidence and love. And I think
that's all you need. As long as you're surrounded by love,
it gives you the confidence to do anything.'
– Heath Ledger

Heath Andrew Ledger was born on 4 April 1979, in Perth's Subiaco Hospital, Australia. His father, Kim, was a mining engineer, while his French teacher mother Sally was descended from Scotland's Campbell clan. Heath would jokingly refer to his forebears as 'the infamous Campbells . . . back then, they were probably criminals!', making light of Australia's heritage as a nation descended from deportees and convicts.

On a parochial level, Kim Ledger had more significant ancestors. The Ledger name was a distinctive part of Perth's history. The family had maintained the Ledger Engineering Foundry, which provided much of the raw material for the famous Perth to Kalgoorlie pipeline. From 1903 it supplied the Western Australian gold fields, and by the 1970s it served over 100,000 people and six million sheep across 44,000 square miles. In more recent times, the Sir Frank Ledger Charitable Trust – named after Heath's philanthropist great-grandfather – was renowned for granting funds to the area's universities, paying for visiting lecturers and funding scholarships for gifted students.

Sally Ledger had named her son after a diminutive of Heathcliff, the central character in Emily Bronte's tragic romantic novel *Wuthering Heights*. (It was her favourite book, and she'd previously named his older sister, Katherine, after the novel's Cathy.) When his son was born, Heath's father was employed at the local auto-racing track where he worked as an engineer, repairing cars. 'Always, always, always gave me trouble,' he later remembered of the boy's earliest years, 'no matter what he did.' But, added Kim, young Heath had always possessed an amazing amount of self-confidence.

Heath followed Katherine to the same Perth school, while they both took advantage of the region's sun, sea and sand. It was a carefree and idyllic early

Heath Ledger photographed in Perth, his hometown.

Left to right: Heath photographed with his great-grandfather and with family members at ages six and ten.

'Sometimes, when you're there it feels like the earth really is flat and you're sitting right on the edge. It's the most isolated city in the world.'
– Heath Ledger on Perth, his hometown

childhood, even if he did not grow up with money, 'or movies or art'. Later in life, he would describe Perth as so far away from anywhere else that 'sometimes, when you're there it feels like the earth really is flat and you're sitting right on the edge. [It is] the most isolated city in the world.' Heath's youthful feelings of isolation – and perhaps even his later melancholia – may be explained by how Perth is geographically closer to Singapore than to Australia's best-known city, Sydney.

Back in his youth, swimming was Heath's best-loved pastime as he learned to snorkel and surf in the nearby sea. Alternatively, he'd spend time with his father at the racetrack, learning all he could about fixing cars. More often his job would consist of simply washing and polishing them to a spectacular shine, rather than anything mechanical. As his father told *Vanity Fair*, 'I was very involved with motor sport and speedway racing. Heath was into go-karts for a certain time and won a few go-kart titles. He was really good at field hockey as well. You get these predetermined ideas: I thought he was going to be on the Olympic field hockey team!'

For his part, Heath wasn't willing to accept the future that appeared to be mapped out for him. 'When I was growing up, my dad put a field hockey stick in my hand,' he'd later admit. While he had no real abiding interest in cars, he also claimed, 'I was prepped to be the next Michael Schumacher!'

At school he was thought of as a pupil more likely to excel as a sportsman than in an academic way, although he was also very good at art. Guildford Grammar School, located on the banks of the Swan River, was a venerable institution where Perth's brightest and best had been taught for over 100 years. Dedicated to 'the growth and freedom of young minds and bodies', it had vast playing fields, horse riding facilities, and even its own farm. Students could row on the river or stretch themselves in an Olympic-sized swimming pool.

Ledger attended the school from year three of his education (in 1987) through

Heath smiles for one of his earliest agency headshots.

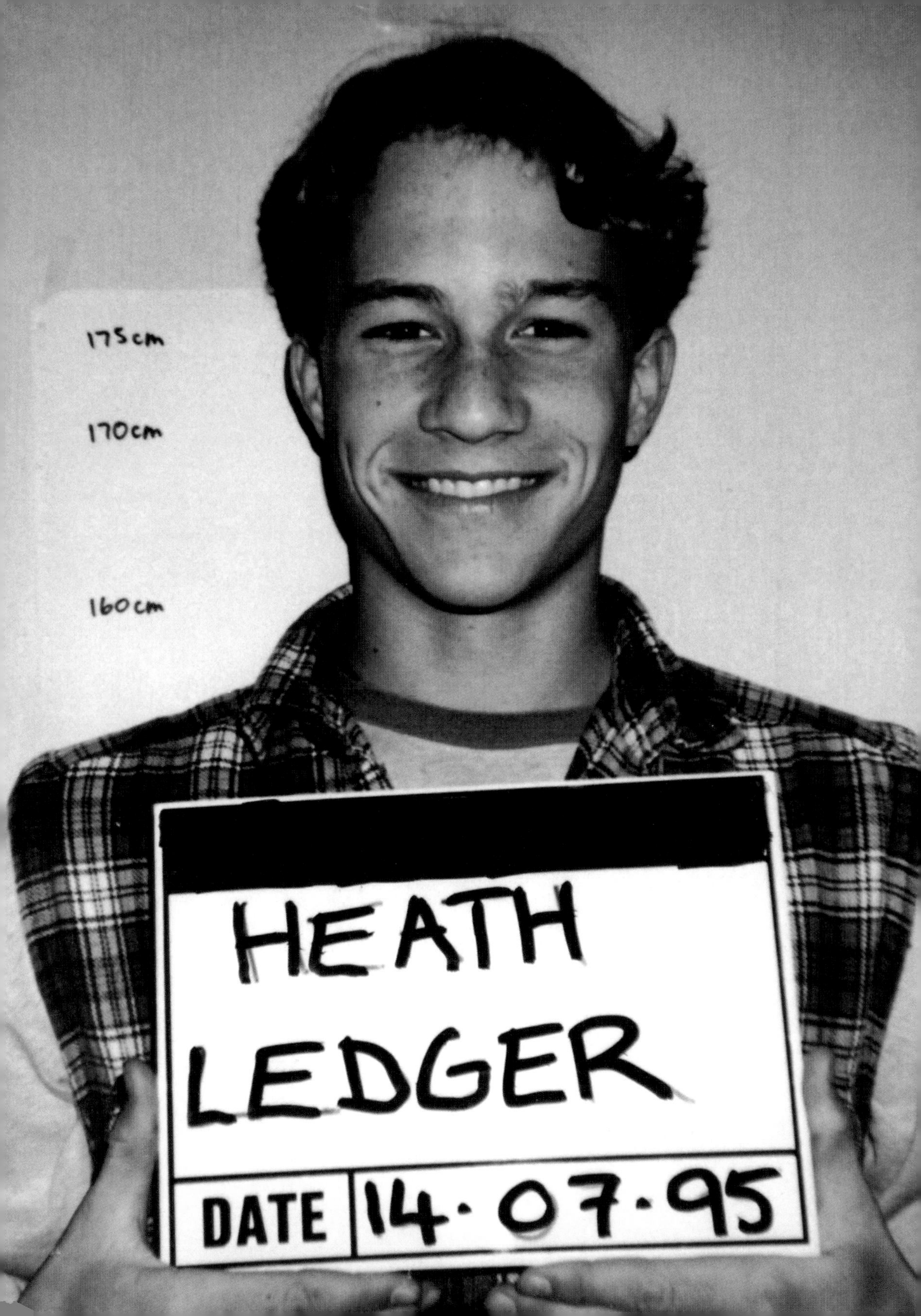
175cm
170cm
160cm
HEATH
LEDGER
DATE 14·07·95

to a few weeks of year twelve (May 1996), before leaving early. He became Captain of Drama in 1996, winning school honours for it, and was year eleven's house monitor. What he lacked academically he more than made up for by being involved in the life of the school.

Field hockey was the other activity that put the young Ledger head and shoulders above his fellow pupils – so much so that he became a small-town school hockey star and won several trophies. 'I don't like telling people I played field hockey,' he later admitted. 'It's real big in Australia for guys, but in America I say I played and everybody goes, "Oh, you girl!"'

Heath was part of the Kalamunda field hockey team in 1990. At high school he was in the first hockey eleven in 1994-5, representing the school in local Public Schools Association tournaments, and played for his home state from 1993-5.

'He worries about everything, from an insect dying onward. He's very soft inside.' – Kim Ledger

The records of the Kalamunda District Hockey Club show the 1990 season started with a new president, Kim Ledger, whose son was playing in the under-thirteens team. Over the 1990 season, young Ledger's team won 21 out of 28 games, with three draws and only four losses. Ledger senior put serious time and effort into attempting to refurbish the club. But by 1992 his plans for new facilities had come to nothing, partly due to rules protecting the habitat of native turtles. Business pressures and disappointment caused Kim to drop out of working for the club – causing his son to lose interest, and a downturn in the club's fortunes over the next few seasons.

Despite his aptitude for hockey and swimming, Heath wouldn't pursue any physical activity just for the sake of it. He actually avoided joining the military cadet programme at Guildford Grammar School. 'You had to wear a uniform,' he later recalled in *Vanity Fair*. 'I didn't want to [prepare to] fight. I thought it was strange that they were teaching kids to shoot automatic weapons. If you didn't do it, they made you play sports. So I played a lot of field hockey, cricket and Australian-rules football. I played them all just to get out of cadets. Who wants to shoot an automatic rifle? What was I going to use that for?'

Kim Ledger fully understood his son's reluctance to take part in the protocols of violence. 'Heath doesn't want to squash an ant,' he said. 'He worries about everything, from an insect dying onward. He's very soft inside. We're the only father and son I know who hug and roll around on the floor of the airport when we meet. We're huggy, touchy people.'

Just as the young Ledger was grateful for the opportunity to engage in extra sports in lieu of learning how to wield a gun, he also had a serious interest in art. He dedicated much time to painting abstract pieces that his doting parents would use to decorate the house, proud of their younger child's endeavours.

'Heath was an arty boy,' recalled Kim. 'He had some of his special abstract paintings pinned on the walls of his room and on the ceiling. We were lying back looking at the art on the ceiling, at about one o'clock in the morning. We'd been

A teenage Heath was all-too aware of the doors a career in acting could open.

'A few teachers at school tried every opportunity to discourage my participation in drama, basically telling me I was wasting my time. That kind of made me angry and determined to prove I could achieve the goals I set for myself.' – Heath Ledger

Left to right: Heath performs in various school productions while still a student at Guildford Grammar.

talking for about half an hour – we often talked like that – I finally told him he was going to have to get some sleep because he had school in the morning. He was about fourteen or fifteen. He said to me, "Well, Dad, you're going to have to get used to this, because this is what I'm going to be doing. I'm going to be very good at it. I'm really going to enjoy it." I always told him that he couldn't be good at anything unless he enjoyed it 150 per cent.' Young Heath's artistic ambitions were clear, even if at this stage he was applying himself to an entirely different art form.

Heath Ledger was also a fan of old movies. He would often while away a Sunday afternoon watching a TV transmission of an old black and white musical with song and dance man Gene Kelly. When asked later how he first got interested in acting, Ledger admitted to *Vanity Fair*, 'It all comes from my love of Kelly. I think he's just awesome. It was more or less the partnership between him and Judy Garland that I liked. There was something so magical about Gene Kelly's films. It was movie-making! They built those amazing sets! They danced and sang!'

Despite this enthusiasm for the performing arts, the younger Ledger wasn't the first to take to the boards. His big sister, Katherine, started performing with local theatre companies while a teenager, including the Globe Shakespeare Company in Perth. Once in a while the younger Ledger would tag along with his sister to an audition, or to watch her in rehearsal, but it was a while before he found himself getting actively interested. When he did start acting in school plays, it was in parts as a sheep and a donkey in a local nativity play. As a fidgety kid who sometimes found it difficult to sit still in class, he was inspired by his hero Gene Kelly to take up modern dance, aiming 'to gain more control over my body. I did some dance courses mainly because when I started doing theatre I was really self-conscious of what my body was doing and where my hands were and what my feet were doing.' Once he got into the swing of it he proved a natural, putting the physical co-ordination developed from swimming and hockey to a new use.

Acting, singing and dancing captured his interest in a way that sports and motor cars just hadn't. However, as Heath took his first tentative steps into the world of theatrical drama, domestic drama was about to enter his family life.

Heath Ledger's escape to the fantasy world of the stage may have been provoked by the end of his parents' relationship, around the age of ten. There was no huge trauma, as his parents split up and found new partners relatively quickly, but the breakup of any family has a disruptive effect. 'I'm sure there was, like, one week where they didn't speak to each other,' he recalled of the separation process. 'I was really cool with it. I was kind of happy about it, actually. I had two houses, two sets of rules. It was wacky. I'd go to one place and when I was sick of that and needed a break I'd go to the other one. It really didn't bother me.'

Heath liked the stage not for the applause, but because it enabled him to escape, to become someone else for a while. Similarly, he'd spend long hours out on the Indian Ocean, solitary surfing on his board, thinking about the changes that were happening in his young life. 'It wasn't the death of something,' Heath later claimed, 'it was the birth of something else.' In some ways, he said, the end of his parents' marriage gave him a new focus in life, forcing him to set a direction for himself, and perhaps to find an outlet for the turmoil he was feeling inside. 'What I've always looked for is redirection of energy and emotion. Maybe the thrust of that started there.'

'I spent a lot of time studying my parents: it's a shortcut to understanding yourself. I gained an early understanding that all human beings are flawed, and it's okay to be flawed, that it's even more interesting.' – Heath Ledger

Both his parents made it clear to their children that they'd remain active in their lives. While that was welcome, it was still an eye-opener for young Ledger. 'You grow up emotionally quicker than other kids, you get more flexible and independent. I spent a lot of time studying my parents: it's a shortcut to understanding yourself. I gained an early understanding that all human beings are flawed, and it's okay to be flawed, that it's even more interesting.'

Moving regularly between both parents' homes gave Heath a new outlook on things. 'That set me off on a gypsy life, excellent training for living out of a bag [as he'd later do as a Hollywood star]. I enjoyed being at one house for three weeks, then going, "Okay, right, I'm off!" It set me up for this bohemian life I've been leading – I feel like I've been travelling with the same bag since I was eleven.'

Both his parents quickly found new partners and over time would start new families, giving him two half-sisters, Ashleigh and Olivia. Eventually, Ledger would sport a tattoo with letters forming the word 'KAOS', for each of his sisters and his mother, Sally. It also reflected his feelings about growing up with the supposed chaos of a lot of women around. 'I learned respect for women, and patience. You grow up with all those women around you . . . you learn to wait your turn.'

At school, Heath was running into trouble with his sports coaches. 'I was a bit of a punk at that age,' he remembered of the end of his junior school days. 'I had a problem with authority.' His coaches felt his timetable of rehearsals and performances was interfering with his field hockey practice. His senior years were looming, so he

'He had a natural ability and enjoyed performing in the school plays, but it's not like he was driven to become a star at that age. I think he started doing it for fun. He had a meteoric rise. He was only a baby when he went to Hollywood.' – Annie Murtagh-Monks

'I started to realise that acting was going to give me more money, and more time off.' – Heath Ledger

Left: *A young and tousled Heath smiles for the camera.*
Above: *Heath's early TV roles quickly propelled him to bigger and better things.*

was faced with a distinct choice: theatre or sport. But if the coaches thought the young Ledger was easy to manipulate, they were wrong. 'A few teachers at school tried every opportunity to discourage my participation in drama, basically telling me I was wasting my time,' he later told his school's website in an interview. 'That kind of made me angry and determined to prove I could achieve the goals I set for myself.'

Early significant performances included the title role in *Peter Pan* and then later, at age fifteen, Laertes in Shakespeare's *Hamlet*. 'I just loved it,' Heath would say of performing, 'so I kept on doing it. I blinked my eyes and I was getting paid. Doors kept opening and I kept walking through them.'

Soon, Heath found himself directing and choreographing his school's entry in the regional Rock Eisteddfod festival. 'It was a nationwide high-school dance competition,' he later explained of what was actually a Celtic festival of the performing arts, established by Welsh settlers. 'You have to create an eight-minute piece to a topic. You have to create your own sets and costumes. Usually a lot of girls' schools do it. We were the first all-guys school to ever do it, and our topic was fashion! I got 60 farm boys who'd never danced before up on stage, and we won! It was cheesy. I choreographed the whole thing, all with farmers at military school . . .' As always, he had an ulterior motive for his dedication: 'We were doing it just to get out of school and go to the competition so we could meet all those girls!'

Heath had a supportive family, willing to back whatever interest he wished to pursue. However, he wasn't coming from a stage background, and neither parent was pushing their kids to act. 'I had to get myself there,' he told *Teen Celebrity* magazine of his early opportunities. '[My parents] were never like a "stage mom" type. It was very much about me finding out who I am, and they never forced opinions on me. That's an amazing thing: I don't know how they did it.'

'I just loved it, so I kept on doing it. I blinked my eyes and I was getting paid. Doors kept opening and I kept walking through them.' – Heath Ledger

At this early stage, there were no serious ambitions to take up acting as a professional endeavour. 'I started to realise that acting was going to give me more money, and more time off,' he later said. 'I didn't really care, though. I was still pretty caught up in just being a teenager. I'm not good at future planning. I don't plan at all. I don't know what I'm doing tomorrow. I completely live in the now, not in the past, not in the future.' At the time, it seemed more likely he'd end up following his father into some kind of practical manual work, like fixing cars. 'It was a hobby,' he'd tell *Teen Celebrity* of his initial efforts in the theatre. 'It was just for fun. I started doing stage acting. I wasn't like a movie brat or anything. I wasn't good enough!' More local productions followed, including major roles in stage adaptations of movies like *In the Name of the Father* and *Bugsy Malone*.

Heath also signed up with an actors' agency; as one of many good looking teenage boys on their books, he was soon winning small parts in TV commercials – often with no lines, just background roles. Ledger didn't mind, he had a longer game-plan. '[Growing] as a person, that's important to my craft,' he later claimed, looking back upon his early acting experiences. 'I did not go to college, so I had to understand who I was before I could start portraying anyone else. As a kid you don't really know who you are. I really wanted to find that out [first]. I don't have a method to my madness . . . For me, acting is more about self-exploration. I've always been very big on self-exploration and answering my own questions. For so many, it's hell growing up. I guess I'm blessed. I've really enjoyed it. I don't let a lot get to me, I really don't.' But Ledger's laidback nature would ultimately not endure the rigours of a career in the public eye.

His first acting mentor was casting agent Annie Murtagh-Monks, who got him his first significant TV and film roles and revels in her reputation as the person who discovered Heath Ledger. After fifteen years as an actress, she'd formed Annie Murtagh-Monks & Associates in 1993, casting commercials, TV series and movies shot in Western Australia. One year later, she would catch the young Heath in his high school production of *Hamlet*. 'He had a natural ability but it wasn't like he was driven to be a star at that age,' she acknowledges of his nascent talent and lack of career-mindedness.

'I'm not good at future planning. I don't plan at all. I don't know what I'm doing tomorrow. I completely live in the now, not in the past, not in the future.'
– Heath Ledger

Speaking to *West Magazine* in 1999, Annie Murtagh-Monks revealed how she launched Heath on his road to acting success. 'Producer [John] Rapsey asked me in 1993 if I would cast a TV series that Barron Films were making.' Besides his theatre work, Heath had featured in a few on-screen roles before he eventually left Perth for Sydney. He appeared in a tiny background role in the 1991 independent Australian kids' film *Clowning Around*, which followed the adventures of foster kid Simon as he tries to become a professional circus clown. Ledger appears in the movie very briefly, dressed as a clown, alongside his future *Blackrock* co-star Rebecca Smart. Next, the then fifteen-year-old Heath won his TV role almost by accident. He'd accompanied elder sister Kate to a meeting with her agent and, through the intervention of Murtagh-Monks, landed a part in Rapsey's TV series, *Ship to Shore*. This children's show revolved around the adventures of a group of kids living on Circe Island, off the coast of Perth. It ran for three series during 1992-4, with Ledger appearing in several later episodes as a character billed as Cyclist.

'I was terrible,' he confessed of his tiny role in *Ship to Shore*, 'but I figured if I could see what I was doing wrong, then I could also fix it.'

Annie Murtagh-Monks then secured him a major role in an ongoing Australian TV series called *Sweat*, in 1995. This was doubly pleasing as it was set at Sports West Academy, a school for hopeful Olympic athletes, so the series allowed him to use his sporty physicality. He'd landed the role of gay teenager Steve 'Snowy' Bowles – seemingly the first portrayal of a gay teen on Australian television, and a performance that prefigured Ledger's acclaimed role in *Brokeback Mountain* many years later.

Originally up for the straightforward leading role of a macho swimming champ, Heath instead opted for the more challenging and controversial part. 'I played a young gay Olympic cycling prospect. It was quite a challenging role for the time,' he told his school's website. His father approved of his risk-taking. 'He had a choice of two roles: one a swimmer, the other a gay bicyclist. I was thinking to myself, "Yeah, he'll choose the swimmer." Then he told me he chose the gay role. His response was it was more of an acting role. "If I want to get some sort of recognition, this is the one I should be doing," he said. He wasn't fazed by any of the other stuff.'

Unlike some mainstream Hollywood actors who avoid playing gay characters (whatever their own sexual orientation), Ledger was more than willing to take on the challenge himself at a young age, as his character came to terms with his own homosexuality. Perhaps it was the fearlessness of youth, or the fact that he knew *Sweat* would be a little-seen TV show. Or maybe he was simply too inexperienced to know the risk he was taking. Either way, he had to stay in top condition as much of his performance featured cycling action.

As creator and writer of the series, John Rapsey said it was clear that Ledger possessed an unusual talent. 'He had absolutely no problem playing the role. He handled all of that with great aplomb. What was noticeable about him was he was concentrated, very quiet, and you could see that he was really observant of other people.'

Sweat ran for 26 hour-long episodes on Australia's Channel 10 through 1996, and introduced Ledger to another young actor who was to become one of his best friends. Martin Henderson, four years older than him, played the role of swimmer Tom Nash, the part Heath was originally offered. The pair would soon be sharing digs as struggling actors in Sydney, after Henderson encouraged him to relocate from Perth.

'I remember just burying my face in my hands thinking, "This is the end, but it hasn't even begun."' – Heath Ledger on *Sweat*

Episode nine of *Sweat* focused on Heath Ledger's character Snowy, as he made attempts to help another gay student battle bullies, before revealing to his friends that he was gay himself. The following episodes featured Snowy's roommate and friend Danny reacting badly to the news of his pal's sexuality, causing Snowy to consider quitting the academy. Danny is so uncomfortable around Snowy he decides he can no longer share a room with him, switching with another student. Later in the series, episode sixteen saw Snowy date another student named Richard, causing him to neglect his cycling and confuse his coach. While none of these soapy storylines was exactly Shakespeare, they were engaging, challenging for their time, and a definite test of young Ledger's growing acting talents.

Viewing his work in *Sweat* when it was first broadcast, however, the young Heath would be less than impressed by his own efforts. 'I was crap,' he remembered of those early performances. 'It was really bad crap. I realised that if I can see that I'm bad, and what I'm doing wrong, why don't I just fix it. If I can see that I'm blinking too much, or not concentrating and recognise it, I'm sure that I should be able to fix it, and that's how it started. The one thing that got me through it was I allowed myself to admit that I was bad.' While he was still in the earliest stages of learning his craft, this doubt about his own abilities would haunt Heath's

Heath's first major TV role was as gay cyclist Snowy Bowles (above left) in Australian teen-drama series Sweat *(1996).*

career. Even when others acclaimed his performances, he himself was never convinced that any individual performance was ever good enough.

'I remember just burying my face in my hands thinking, "This is the end, [but] it hasn't even begun,"' he said of *Sweat*. His reactions showed the first signs of the obsessive perfectionism that would come to weigh heavily on Ledger's mind, even as he found success in Hollywood.

He consulted his mother, Sally, to see what she thought. 'She just said, "Well, that's okay." The honesty kind of slipped out of her, in the most beautiful way. She didn't even bother with "No, honey, you were great, I'm so proud of you." No one else around you, except your mum, is going to tell you that you suck. She straight-up told me: "There are other things to do in life." The work I did on TV in Australia was crap. My mum and dad were the first to laugh about it. They never thought I was going to make it [as an actor].'

With determination, Heath graduated from Guildford Grammar School a year early, securing his high school diploma by the age of sixteen. 'I got my marks and fucked off,' he said, bluntly. In a way, by forcing his hand his school had made the choice for him. The teenaged Heath Ledger had decided it would be an actor's life for him. Out of school, and with the beginnings of an acting résumé, he had a total of just 69 cents to call his own. Despite that, he felt it was time to live his life to the full. '[I felt] the train of life was just flying by and I had to get on it. It wasn't so much about a career: I wanted to pursue life! I wanted to feel pain, experience love and emotions, all of that. [I wanted to] grow as a person.'

To that end, Heath decided he had to borrow some cash from his parents and leave his hometown of Perth behind, as he'd been encouraged to do by Martin Henderson. 'I jumped in a car and drove to Sydney, with my best mate, Trevor [DiCarlo],' he remembered much later. 'It's a long drive [around 3000 miles] and it's one straight road with nothing between. It only took a few months – but that's still a long time when you're living on nothing! I've known Trevor since I was three, and we haven't spent two months apart. He's like my brother. He now works as my PA.'

It was a big step for a sixteen-year-old to take. 'I'm so amazed and respectful of the fact that my parents let me follow my dream. They were completely open for me to discover things myself. I have a wonderful relationship with them: they're like best friends of mine. I'm sure they were worried, and I'm sure they did mind, but I was going to go regardless. I think they knew that. I've always been very stubborn, so they had the choice of going with me and being my friend or becoming my enemy and saying: "Don't go." They knew that, so they said: "Okay, good luck."'

'He was a student at Guildford Grammar. I saw him performing there, and I was casting *Sweat*, and that's when we first asked him to audition. He had an amazing natural ability to connect imaginatively.' – Annie Murtagh-Monks

Kim Ledger wasn't surprised by his son's decision, but that didn't mean he entirely approved. 'He does seem to have a destiny that he's in charge of. Heath took off at a very early age. He's barely been home since then,' he later told *Vanity Fair*. But his father wasn't as sanguine about it as the younger Ledger seemed to think. 'It broke my heart. We spent our life together playing sports. [As a parent] you participate in everything they do. So when they take off, it's like a divorce.' Hurt though he was by his son's move to Sydney, his father knew the boy would do okay. 'Though he's a fairly laidback kid, he's also pretty streetwise.'

And he was ambitious. Unsure of how he was going to make his way as an actor, it was inevitable that he would head for the bright lights. 'It wasn't that hard to leave and head for Sydney,' he said. 'Not at that age. No matter how good your family is, you just want out. I had to move on. I could have just sat on the beach and painted really bad paintings, writing really bad poetry and surfed really great waves. It's the ethic of the aboriginal ideal, the ideal of the "walkabout". You take off by yourself, and gather knowledge from other lands and other tribes, and then you bring it back to your family, explain your stories, what you've learned and how you've grown.'

Ledger soon arrived at Mark Henderson's place in Sydney with little luggage and his precious surfboard. Eventually, he, Henderson and Trevor DiCarlo would share a flat on Bondi Beach for about a year.

Heath had already made one major decision: acting school just wouldn't be his style. 'I never studied acting in Australia. I never had an empty stage and black pyjamas to run around and express myself. I feared four years in acting academy would spit me out like a Toyota model with a set of rules, when I felt acting was about defying rules.' As a non-academic who refused to submit either to authority figures or several more years of institutionalised education, he could never have been hidebound by rules. '. . . I've made all my mistakes on film. I need a space where I can just sit and think and find a voice for the character and visualise it. I've learned a lot about myself in order to learn about the craft.' For Heath Ledger, learning on the job would be the way forward. All he had to do now was win some roles.

His first big movie break came in 1996, the same year in which he'd moved to Sydney. Heath won the role of a surfer named Toby Ackland in an Australian teen film called *Blackrock*. Written by Nick Enright (who previously wrote the weepie *Lorenzo's Oil*) from his own play and directed by Australian TV actor Steven Vidler, it chronicled the consequences for a group of surfer friends when a local girl is raped and murdered by one of them. As the details of the crime emerge and the degree of the various boys' involvement is revealed, their friendships are tested to destruction. Heath's was very much a supporting role.

Released on 1 May 1997, *Blackrock* was a minor local success, grossing over $A1 million, but was little seen outside its native country. *Variety* did post a critical review following a screening at the January 1997 Sundance Film Festival, calling it 'dulled by stilted dialogue' and 'weakened by a TV cop-drama approach'. This early in his career, Heath did not stand out among the cast. The film did score several local award nominations, though.

Following *Blackrock*, Ledger played the small role of Oberon, Shakespeare's King of the Fairies from *A Midsummer Night's Dream*, in a play sequence within an Australian children's film called *Paws*. Featuring veteran Scottish comic Billy Connolly as the voice of a dog called PC, the plot centred on various characters searching for a hidden $1 million, with clues on a computer disc given to the smarter-than-average dog. The movie was appealing enough to younger children to gross £1.7 million on release in the UK between February and April 1998, and *Variety* dubbed it an 'enjoyable doggy film . . . generally on the button for the pubescent crowd'.

Heath's roles in *Blackrock* and *Paws* were too insignificant to even gain a mention. It's probably just as well, as he wasn't taking his craft too seriously at this stage. 'When I was making those [early] roles, I was really youthful and careless,' he later told *The New York Daily News*. 'I didn't even really care about performance: it was silly and commercial, and I would [have felt] way too concerned with myself if I took it seriously. Where the film was shot was more appealing to me than what it was [about]. I was more concerned with having a good time than with focusing on work . . . All I saw were mistakes: a lack of care, lack of attention to detail.' This ambivalent attitude to his work would sow the seeds of the obsessive attention to detail and psychological realism he brought to his later roles – at the cost of intense psychological pressure in his off-screen life.

Heath also featured in a few 1997 episodes of the long-running Australian TV soap *Home and Away*, as Scott Irwin, the boyfriend of Sally Fletcher (Kate Ritchie, an actress who virtually grew up on the show). Having chronicled the lives of the

Cruel school newcomer Scott (Heath) torments Sally (Kate Ritchie) in a 1997 episode of long-running Australian soap Home and Away.

residents of Summer Bay in New South Wales for almost a decade back then, *Home and Away* had proven (alongside *Neighbours*) to be a training ground for a whole generation of young Australian actors. Unsurprisingly perhaps, Heath Ledger was the latest to pass through its revolving doors. In episodes 2158 to 2168, earring-wearing bad boy Scott encourages Sally's attentions simply so he can steal a modern studies exam paper from the school office. A drunken party on the beach follows, and Sally is seen running from a van the next morning after having earlier gone inside with Scott. Ashamed of her behaviour (the implication is they've had sex, whereas Sally was probably a virgin before), Sally turns Scott into the school authorities. This leads to him bullying Sally, even framing her for another theft, before he's found out and the character's story comes to an end with him being expelled. Other low-key TV guest appearances at this time included turns in children's drama series *Bush Patrol*, set in the Katta-Moornda National Park, and sitcom *Corrigan*.

While the Australian film industry would occasionally flourish, it was not easy for an actor to secure one of the limited number of big roles available. However, there was a boom in TV production in Australia for series aimed at the US market, as it was a cheaper location in which to shoot than the US. For any struggling actor, the secure income from a regular TV gig is obviously very welcome. It was for this reason that Heath Ledger was soon playing the lead in a TV show called *Roar!*, starting in 1997.

Following the likes of New Zealand-based heroic fantasy shows *Xena: Warrior Princess* and *Hercules: The Legendary Journeys*, *Roar!* was set in a legendary (and far from historically accurate) version of Ireland in 400 AD. Ledger played Conor, an orphaned Celtic prince out to rid his land of invading Roman hordes. (In actuality, the Romans invaded Britain but not Ireland.) His task is to unite the warring Celtic clans while drawing on the wisdom and support of his mystical advisor Galen (Norman Kaye), teenage troublemaker Tully (Alonzo Greer), beautiful former slave girl Caitlin (Vera Farmiga) and warrior Fergus (John Saint Ryan). Standing against them is the villain Longinus (Sebastian Roche), a seemingly normal 30-year-old Centurion who is, in reality, evil Queen Diana's (Lisa Zane) 400-year-old sorceror, who stabbed Christ with the Spear of Destiny during the crucifixion and was cursed with eternal life.

Roar! first aired on the US Fox network in July 1997. It was created by Shaun Cassidy (half-brother of 1970s teen heartthrob David Cassidy), who at various stages was also involved in such successful TV series as *Cold Case*, *The Agency*, *American Gothic* and *Invasion*. Cassidy teamed up with *Beauty and the Beast* creator Ron Koslow to bring that series' combination of fairy tale, romance and action-adventure to an ancient historical setting, in the style of *Xena* and *Hercules*.

'I've made all my mistakes on film,' Heath claimed of his early start in the industry.

The strange title of the show received an equally odd explanation on the series' official website: 'What's at stake for Conor and his people is the "Roar": the roar of the land, the roar of the people – a voice that echoes through every living thing and is the power of life.' To many, it sounded like a knockoff of *Star Wars'* mythic 'Force', and there's a moment in the first episode in which Conor is told by Galen to 'remember all we are and all that's come before and hear the roar . . . the voice that echoes in every living thing, the power that binds us together.'

The first order of business for Cassidy was to find a leading man who displayed the qualities of a Lucy Lawless (*Xena*) or Kevin Sorbo (*Hercules*), but could stand alone as the king of the mythic Celtic peoples. 'Heath was a complete unknown, but everybody fell in love with him,' remembered Tom Thayer, former president of Universal Television, talking to *Entertainment Weekly*. 'He was very green, but he

had raw energy and this incredible charm.'

Recalled Cassidy, 'We needed a young man who had the strength of a much older man. I tried to cast out of New York, Los Angeles and Ireland, but all the seventeen-to-nineteen-year-olds sounded like they just walked out of a shopping mall. Heath had a maturity and a commanding presence.' Talking at the time of Ledger's Oscar nomination for *Brokeback Mountain*, Cassidy recalled casting the young actor. 'I think I gave him his first job. I know I gave him his first plane ticket to America. I saw him on video when he was seventeen or eighteen and Ron Koslow and I put him on an airplane. He came out to LA and we tested him. He got the part and he was great. Everybody thought he was going to be a big star.' Having enjoyed a brief career as a pop star and a role in *The Hardy Boys/Nancy Drew Mysteries* in 1977, Cassidy could see what potentially lay ahead for Heath Ledger.

For his part, Heath knew very little about Shaun Cassidy's TV work. 'I knew about the 1970s teen idol thing, mainly from my mom,' he later remembered. 'I read the description of the show, and I said to myself, "This sounds dodgy!" But when I learned more about it, my heart was in it.'

'I never studied acting in Australia. I feared four years in acting academy would spit me out like a Toyota model with a set of rules, when I felt acting was about defying rules.'
– Heath Ledger

According to Cassidy, 'Heath was probably the youngest actor we saw. We'd envisioned Conor as a 22- or 23-year-old guy, but Heath changed our minds. You have to believe that he's a boy who's still got a lot to learn. When the chips are down, he's going to stand up in front of people who are a lot older and say, "I'm in charge and you are going to follow me." And he's got that quality.'

Ledger was flown out to Los Angeles to film a screen test in front of studio executives. When he arrived, he was so jetlagged and nervous that he blundered his way through. It was to be the first of several bad experiences with auditions in America, and Heath was convinced he had blown his chance. 'The room was packed with suits,' he remembered. 'After every shot, they swarmed together like a pack of ants on a sweet biscuit, whispering. It was definitely not my best performance, but something must have gone right.'

Ledger's perverse lack of faith in his own abilities gave him the mistaken impression he'd failed the audition. But now he had to get to grips with the character of Conor, and the Irish accent that went with it. 'This show is based on passion,' he told *Access Hollywood*, in an onset video interview. 'I think that'll stand out against a lot of other shows. [Galen takes Conor] to a special cliff where he hears the "roar". This "roar" is a sound, a feeling that comes from the Earth. It is telling him to forget his own need for revenge. The "roar" that we're trying to show is an inner strength. He's to lead this group of people whom Galen has collected together, who've lost their families. That spurs him on. It's an inspirational moment for him, the pivotal scene of the series.'

Heath seemed to recognise that *Roar!* was nonsense, but, given it was his first

In the TV series Roar! *(1997) Heath landed a lead role as orphaned Celtic prince Conor.*
'It wasn't seen by many people – or at least, not by the right people,' the young actor would later observe.

major showcase for American audiences, he was prepared to take it seriously. 'The series was shortlived, but it did give me excellent exposure in the US. I did a lot of background research for it. I read up on Celtic lore, druidism and things like that. I had to spend a lot of time by myself – it sounds like the cliché actor thing – to find the character, but I really had to sit down and find this guy. Conor is a very special character: he's a hero, but he's not a hero that gets everything right.'

Playing the lead meant a punishing schedule, but he was willing to put up with it if it allowed him to make his mark. 'I'm very proud to have the opportunity to be in such a show as this. Every day, it is not a hassle getting up out of bed at three o'clock in the morning and coming home at ten o'clock at night. When my family see it, I'm sure they'll be overwhelmed. It's a bonus to be shooting in Australia . . . it's a lot more relaxing.'

'I believed I could be an actor and I left home at an early age to pursue that dream. My father and mother thought I was committing suicide. It wasn't until I started earning money that they finally understood I was secure and safe. It is hard to convince anyone of your hopes and dreams until you manifest them and prove them.' – Heath Ledger

Universal made *Roar!* on Queensland's Gold Coast, where there was a growing film and TV production base. Heath learned many practical skills while making the show that would pay off in later roles – specifically horse riding and sword fighting, which he would later use variously in *A Knight's Tale*, *The Patriot* and *Brokeback Mountain*. ('My dad was able to rent a house on the edge of a national forest for cheap if we fed the horses,' he recalled of a childhood experience – although up until making the show, he'd never actually ridden a horse.)

Altogether he spent seven months on the Gold Coast. Assistant director Stuart Freeman – veteran of such Australian productions as *Mad Max Beyond Thunderdome*, *Dead Calm* and *Priscilla, Queen of the Desert* – remembered Heath as a generous and enthusiastic young actor. 'When I met him he was a handsome, fresh-faced star and we just knew he would go far . . . The media say he went straight from Perth to Hollywood, but it was really here that Heath honed his skills.'

Stunt coordinator Danny Baldwin worked with him on his horse riding and fighting skills. 'He was a quick learner and by the end of filming he could ride bareback with a sword. He was probably the most talented actor I've worked with. Heath was an absolute sweetheart.'

But as with so many of his early projects, Ledger was not entirely happy with *Roar!* as a finished product. 'It started off quite dignified and *Braveheart*-esque,' the actor said in a 2006 *Rolling Stone* profile, 'but as they got desperate for ratings, slowly no one's wearing clothes. I'm like, "Why is there a gang of bikini models fighting?"'

Fox promised producer Shaun Cassidy that, if the show reached a big enough audience, the network would order a further 22 episodes. 'We believe people might like to see something fresh and original right now,' said Cassidy, 'and hopefully we can gain a foothold that will carry us into the fall.'

But unfortunately the reviews were scathing. *Variety* dubbed it 'the most

Although Roar! *was both short-lived and critically derided, it raised Heath's international profile significantly.*

shamelessly derivative hour in recent network history,' while calling Heath a 'blond-tressed, pinup-worthy hero' whose 'Irish brogue tends to come and go, rather like the wind.' *Entertainment Weekly*'s Ken Tucker called Ledger a 'cutie-pie with a fetching little blond braid hanging down the right side of his face. Heath Ledger looks not a little like a Celtic version of [Shaun] Cassidy during the latter's teen idol days . . . a knockabout Australian . . . handsome and muscular in a refreshingly non-bodybuilder way, though too lightweight to pull off the sort of lamentations for his freedom that the producers regularly crib from Mel Gibson and *Braveheart*.' The *New York Times* called the show 'unintentionally laughable . . . a mix of mystical mumbo jumbo and high school chic . . . a hopeless mix of earnest content and cheesy trappings', but singled out Heath as the series' saving grace: '*Roar!* has only two chances for success: Ledger, who is being carefully positioned as a heartthrob (the little blond braid hanging over his right ear serves as a ready-made trademark), will have to come through in that role; or this series will have to embrace its inner kitsch.'

But the ratings simply didn't meet expectations, and after screening only eight of the thirteen episodes Fox and Universal cancelled the show. 'It was a thirteen-week experiment,' Ledger told *Teen Celebrity*. 'It wasn't seen by many people – or at least, not by the right people – in America.'

However, while it was not a success with the general audience in the way that *Xena* and *Hercules* had been, *Roar!* did find a loyal and vocal fan following

(including some who wrote reams of fan fiction inspired by the series), who managed to campaign for the release of the complete series on DVD in 2006. Following Heath Ledger's death, *TV Guide* would even say of his performance: '[It is] a shining example of a young star just starting to take shape. As Conor, Ledger simply commands the screen, which is no small feat, considering he was going up against legions of warring Celts and some funky Christian-Druid mythology. But honestly, nobody could set their jaw like that kid.'

Apart from the professional exposure, Heath would have one more reason to be grateful to *Roar!*. On the series he met actress Lisa Zane, brother of *Titanic* star Billy. She played Conor's nemesis, Queen Diana, but unlike their screen counterparts the actors seriously hit it off. With both of them far away from home – Perth and Sydney in Heath's case, the even more distant US with Lisa – they found love on the Gold Coast.

Their romantic liaison would set the template for several of the young actor's future relationships, with Zane about eighteen years his senior. (She was born in 1961, he in 1979.) On the set of *Roar!* Heath and Lisa were inseparable, but their romance would also prove somewhat short-lived. It did serve to bring the actor back to America, however.

'I don't have a method to my madness . . . For me, acting is more about self-exploration. I've always been very big on self-exploration and answering my own questions.' – Heath Ledger

'I didn't think I was just going to turn up in Hollywood and get work,' he later admitted. 'I was in love at the time I did *Roar!*, dating a girl in the show. When she went back to LA, I had to go with her. I lived with her for two years and stayed there with her.'

Following his arrival in California in late 1997, Ledger endured four months of fruitless meetings with agents until finally scoring an appointment with the big one: Creative Artists Agency (CAA), Hollywood's biggest players. 'He had all the characteristics of a man,' recalls CAA agent Steve Alexander, 'and yet he was a boy. But you could just feel that there was something important going on right away. Everyone who met him had that impression of him.'

Yet, despite Alexander taking him under his wing, prime Stateside parts were not forthcoming. Just as things were looking bleak, opportunity knocked in the most perverse way. 'I wasn't getting anything in Australia, so I'd moved to LA,' he later recalled. 'Then, the first gig I got was *Two Hands*, back in Australia! I had to go to LA for them to say: "Oh, come back home." They think you're a bigger actor if you're in LA. You know: "He can afford the ticket, he must be doing okay."'

Having paid his dues in Australian TV, notched up a couple of minor film roles and won the lead in a short-lived American TV series, Heath Ledger had finally decided he was ready for the big time in Hollywood. But Hollywood wasn't yet ready for him, and the first role he scored put him on a plane right back to the land of his birth.

'You could just feel that there was something important going on right away,' said Heath's agent, Steve Alexander, of their first meeting. 'Everyone who met him had that impression of him.'

2. HOLLYWOOD CALLS

'You've got to realise the power of saying "No." It's what
you say "Yes" to that ultimately shapes you. One way I manage
is to not take the film industry completely seriously while at the
same time taking my craft seriously. There is a life outside
acting, I won't let it overtake my life.'
– Heath Ledger

Heath Ledger's first lead role in a movie returned him from Hollywood to his native Australia. Director Gregor Jordan cast him as the central character in crime comedy-drama *Two Hands*, having decided he was the only actor for the part. 'I was lucky to have found Heath Ledger at a time when he was available and I could still afford him,' admitted Jordan. 'He was just on the verge of taking off. And we just hit it off – we became very good friends.'

Ledger featured as nineteen-year-old Jimmy, a lowlife criminal recruited as courier for a mob boss and drug kingpin called Pando, played by established Australian star Bryan Brown. Hoping to win the respect of his peers, Jimmy makes a fundamental mistake when he's distracted by a pretty girl on the beach while carrying $A10,000 of Pando's cash. Hiding the envelope stuffed with cash in the sand, Jimmy takes a dip in the sea. While he's gone, young street kids Helen (Mariel McClorey) and Pete (Evan Sheaves) – who'd been surreptitiously watching him – steal the money. Returning to the beach, Jimmy is distraught. Soon, Pando has ordered a hit on him, believing the kid stole the money. Can Jimmy make good on the debt by stepping up his criminal activities and pulling off a bank job? Or can the love of Alex (Rose Byrne) rescue him from his criminal path?

This was a strong central role for an actor of Ledger's growing experience and obvious talent. And *Two Hands* wasn't simply a straightforward crime drama, either. Gregor Jordan wrote his first feature inspired by a love of modern American gangster films, like *The Godfather* and *GoodFellas*. Aware that, ever since *Reservoir Dogs*, macho crime thrillers were in vogue, 'The story evolved into a black comedy gangster film, with a supernatural subplot,' explained Jordan. 'It is, however, very Australian and that's what makes it different.' It also had a strong

Blonde ambition. Heath knew that if he was going to get ahead in Hollywood, compromises would have to be made.

element of the supernatural, with an occasional voiceover from Jimmy's dead older brother (played by Steven Vidler, director of *Blackrock*) as a kind of guardian angel returned from Hell, and an amusing vein of character-led situation comedy running through it. But while it would make for a colourful local gangster flick, the supernatural content seemed to throw non-Australian audiences. 'The Man – Jimmy's older brother – has dug his way out of Hell to try and prevent Jimmy from taking the same path in life,' explained Vidler of his living dead character. 'I pop up every now and then to chat to the audience and to tell them what's happening.'

As first visualised, an upcoming young actor like Heath Ledger would never have been in the frame to play Jimmy. 'Originally I had written the character as a 30-year-old, but it didn't make sense for a 30-year-old to make so many stupid mistakes,' said Jordan. 'So Jimmy became a young, naïve, but passionate nineteen-year-old, which makes a lot more sense. As I was writing the role, I knew I was going to have a problem finding an actor to play it. Most actors aren't very experienced at that age and this needed to be someone who could carry the film, and play a character who was tough, but at the same time very charismatic.'

Then, one of several casting agents working on the movie drew Jordan's attention to Ledger. 'People were coming back from the shoot of this US series, *Roar!*, in Queensland, and saying, "Wow, take a look at this Heath Ledger."' Jordan obtained an early copy of an episode, 'and within ten seconds I knew he was right for Jimmy. I needed a nineteen-year-old with enough charisma to carry the film and also with enough technical skills so he wouldn't be a nightmare to shoot with.'

'Within ten seconds I knew he was right for Jimmy. I needed a nineteen-year-old with enough charisma to carry the film and also with enough technical skills so he wouldn't be a nightmare to shoot with.' – Gregor Jordan

By this time, of course, the shooting of *Roar!* was history and Ledger was in LA, hoping to win a part in an American movie. A screen test was arranged for *Two Hands*, and Jordan even flew to the US himself to win over his number one choice. 'We hung out together for a week or so, talked about the film and generally had a great time.' As with Martin Henderson on *Sweat*, their professional meeting led to the beginning of an abiding personal friendship that, in turn, resulted in Ledger taking the lead role in *Ned Kelly* for Jordan several years later.

Jordan's screenplay for *Two Hands* stood out from the many generic American movies Heath was then reading for. 'I thought the script was really interesting because it is about current day Australian gangsters, and I don't think that's ever been done before. Jimmy was one of the best characters I'd read because he goes through so much, both love and pain. In addition to all the action, there's a real love story going on between Jimmy and Alex.' As a bonus, there was even a bank robbery scene. ('He gets to rob a bank – I've always wanted to rob a bank!')

Confirming how their friendship began, Ledger admitted it was Jordan, as much as the role itself, that convinced him to return so suddenly to Australia. 'Gregor was one of the few directors that I really connected with. I loved working

Beyond acting, photography was one of Heath's primary artistic pursuits.

'Heath is incredibly generous and has a huge heart. He's a real people person and fits into any situation or any group of people.'
– Rose Byrne, Heath's *Two Hands* co-star

Left: Put 'em up. Jimmy (Heath) prepares to stand his ground after losing $10,000 of mob boss Pando's (Bryan Brown) cash.
Above: The naïve Jimmy contemplates his life-or-death predicament.

with him, I really did. We both had the same ideas about what would work and what wouldn't, but it was something we didn't ever need to discuss. We just knew.'

Making *Two Hands* would prove an education for Heath Ledger. Not least because, in his co-star Bryan Brown, he found something close to a role model. 'I'm a huge fan,' claimed Ledger of the respected Australian actor. 'His work has always inspired me – he was one of the reasons I wanted to be an actor in the first place. I was thrilled and excited to work with him. I discovered that not only is he a very fine actor, he's also a great guy.' (Brown is best known to audiences outside Australia as Tom Cruise's co-star in *Cocktail*, and for the two *F/X* thrillers.)

That wet autumn of April 1998 (seasons are reversed down under), Heath found himself shooting *Two Hands* in familiar locations across Sydney, from the low-rent district of Kings Cross to semi-rural Ingleside, from his old haunts in Bondi Beach to the leafy suburb of Terrey Hills. An empty building in Revesby stood in for the fictional Australian Mutual Bank, site of the comically bungled robbery, while the ensuing car chase was shot in Parramatta Road in Homebush, a familiar location often used for film and TV productions shot in Sydney.

'All the great actors have this "thing". It's difficult to define. Even before Heath was famous, people would pay him a lot of attention. It's something that's totally separate from actual acting.' – Gregor Jordan

It was an odd homecoming for the rising star, but it allowed him to slip easily into character. 'Jimmy goes on such a roller-coaster of a ride – he really hits everything from love to violence to pain,' said Heath. 'He's grown up in and around the Cross, so he's never really known any other life than the one of crime. It's Alex who opens up a whole new world for him and helps him to see that there is a better way to live.'

Two Hands received broadly favourable reviews. 'Clever, hip and razor sharp,' said *Rolling Stone*. But it was *Film Australia* who noted how Ledger 'struts his stuff so confidently that there is absolutely no doubt we will be seeing much of him in the future.' In critic Shaun de Waal's prophetic words: 'Mark my words: Heath Ledger will soon be as big as Brad Pitt or Keanu Reeves.'

Two Hands didn't travel well beyond Australia, however, its cultural references and dialogue too specific for international audiences. 'Australians have a huge slang which Americans just would not understand,' Heath said to *Detour* magazine. 'It's not that they didn't want to get it, it's that they just can't. It just didn't work.' A case in point was a screening at the independent Sundance Film Festival. The half-dozen Australians in the audience clearly 'got' the movie, laughing out loud at the appropriate points, but Ledger recalled nothing but silence from the Americans. Consequently, the film failed to secure a theatrical distributor in the US (although it was eventually available on DVD).

Still, the Australian Film Institute nominated Heath for their Best Actor in a Leading Role award for *Two Hands*. Although he didn't win, it served to raise the young actor's profile both within the industry and with the public. Now, to take the crucial next step, he had to leave Australia once more . . .

Even as Heath made his first waves in Hollywood,
he found time to ride the ocean tides to which he was more accustomed.

Heath had missed Lisa Zane while he was back in Sydney. However, it quickly became apparent that a long-distance relationship suited neither of them. Comfortably back on home turf, he was soon romancing Melbourne model Christina Cauchi. 'The only thing I will say is that I am madly, truly in love and extremely happy. I'm not saying anything else,' Heath said to the *Herald Sun*. In the short-term, the relationship wouldn't last – but they'd hook up again about a year later, when they were both living in New York.

Having not yet reached his twentieth birthday, it must have been tempting for Heath Ledger to think about staying in Australia after coming back from LA for his first starring role. *Two Hands* had yet to be released, and he had no idea whether it would launch him onto a whole new career in Australian film. He also had his extended family locally – but he had a whole new potential career waiting for him back in LA. Decision time was looming for the young actor.

'I loved *The Taming of the Shrew* and always wanted to play Petruchio, and this was the closest thing I could get.' – Heath

Ledger was also having his first brushes with the media at this time, learning how to field questions and answer trivia. But some questions were more pertinent to his state of mind. Asked whether he thought *Two Hands* would help his career, he was honest: 'I don't know, because the only time I ever really think about where my life is going or what direction it's taking me is when people ask me questions like that!'

As he became ever more famous, the media would become a larger, more problematic part of his life. But back then, Heath Ledger was the sex symbol of many adoring female fans who'd watched him on *Roar!* And he seemed to be having second thoughts about the need to make it big in American movies. Asked if he thought it was important for Australian actors to go overseas, he hinted at his inner confusion: 'No it's not important,' he claimed, as though trying to persuade himself of his own opinion. 'It depends if it's important to you to be big or not. You just follow however or wherever life takes you.' Luckily for Heath, the decision was made for him when he was summoned urgently to an audition in the US, mere weeks after wrapping on *Two Hands*.

It is often said that every actor expects to test him – or herself by playing a role in Shakespeare. (For young men, the prime part is that of Hamlet.) Throughout the 1990s, there had been a stream of mainstream movies that adapted the Bard into the present day. Ever since the success of Baz Lurhmann's *Romeo and Juliet*, starring Leonardo DiCaprio and Claire Danes, there had also been a vogue for teenager-focused romantic comedies drawn from classic plays or novels, including 1995's *Clueless* (based on Jane Austen's *Emma*), and 1999's *Cruel Intentions* (a teen version of *Dangerous Liaisons*). *10 Things I Hate About You* was merely the latest in line, a very loose retelling of Shakespeare's *The Taming of the Shrew*.

Director Gil Junger was wary of the project to begin with. 'My agent said it was a high school comedy based on *Taming of the Shrew*. I said, "Absolutely not,"'

Patrick (Heath) contends with the shrewish Kat (Julia Stiles) in hit teen comedy 10 Things I Hate About You *(1999).*

remembered the former TV sitcom director. 'I had no interest in doing a typical high school film. At the urging of my agent, I read the script. The depth of it surprised me. It really is a romantic love story. The plot is beautifully interwoven and the humour works, because it comes from the characters.'

With Junger on board and the script locked down, casting looked set to be a straightforward process. 'My goal was to cast really good actors and not necessarily stars,' said Junger. 'When I finally made my decisions of who I wanted for the roles, there was no question in my mind. Immediately after reading each of the eight chosen actors, I knew right then and there that I didn't need to see anyone else.'

Junger may have been convinced, but the film's producers were not so taken with his choice for the leading role of Patrick Verona. They convinced Junger to consider one more actor, very late in the pre-production process. It was this last-minute indecision that brought Heath into the frame.

'My first reaction to Heath Ledger was, "This guy is great looking, I hope he can act,"' remembers Junger. 'When I talked with him I realised how bright he was. Then he read for me, and after about three minutes and 40 seconds, I knew that he was the right actor for the role. There was initial concern over Heath's Australian accent, but I said, "Why? It makes him more interesting, mysterious and sexy."'

Heath returned to the United States to co-star in *10 Things I Hate About You*, removing his sense of indecision – at least temporarily. There was a problem, though. As Ledger's casting had been a last-minute decision, he was joining a film

'I'm not usually a singer, but I was a singer that day.
I felt like a rock star.' – Heath on *10 Things*' infamous
'Can't Take My Eyes Off Of You' sequence

'Heath is a great actor. There is some interesting chemistry between us.'
– Julia Stiles

Left: *All-singing, all-dancing. High school lothario Patrick serenades Kat.*
Above: *Patrick hatches a plot with Michael (David Krumholz) and Cameron (Joseph Gordon-Levitt).*
Below: *Kat and Patrick share a tender moment.*

that had already undergone a rehearsal period and was due to start principal photography just two days after he touched down in Hollywood. 'I didn't know anyone,' he recalled of turning up on set. 'I'd just come straight off *Two Hands* in Sydney and I wasn't there for rehearsals. . .' Luckily, he knew the film's source material. 'I loved *The Taming of the Shrew* and always wanted to play Petruchio, and this was the closest thing I could get.'

This rewrite of *The Taming of the Shrew* not only drew from that play but also made wider reference to the Shakespearean canon, all in the guise of a teen romantic comedy. In the movie, the Stratford sisters, Bianca (Larisa Oleynik) and Kat (Julia Stiles), have a mutual problem. Their gynaecologist father Walter (Larry Miller) won't allow pretty and popular Bianca to date until her older sister has got herself a boyfriend. However, Kat is an abrasive, quick-tempered sourpuss, the school's social outcast. Cameron (Joseph Gordon-Levitt) knows that if he's to succeed with Bianca, he must first set up Kat with a boyfriend.

'When we read together, there was an instant spark. We were just firing back at each other. We saw it in our eyes.' – Heath Ledger on *10 Things* co-star Julia Stiles

With help from his buddies Michael (David Krumholz) and Joey (Andrew Keegan) he bribes moody newcomer Patrick (Ledger) to take Kat out. A romantic comedy of errors set among the rituals of American high school follows, as Joey comes to believe that Bianca is interested in him, while Kat and Patrick's fake romance blossoms into the real thing. However, when Kat learns of the way she's been set up, things take a dramatic and emotional turn.

'Basically, Patrick Verona is an adaptation of the classic character Petruchio,' explained Heath. 'I'm using bits and pieces of Richard Burton's portrayal of that character in perhaps the best-known *The Taming of the Shrew* film, but my Patrick has also got a Jack Nicholson edge to him with his cheekiness and his smiles. I always wanted to play Hamlet, but I would not attempt it until I was ready. Of all Shakespeare's characters, I'd choose to play Petruchio first.'

In the movie, Patrick returns to Padua High School after a year-long absence. Theories abound as to where he's been and what he's been up to. 'He uses the rumours about him to create a barrier that keeps him isolated from everyone else,' said Ledger. 'Then he meets someone who has also separated herself and together, we break down each other's barriers and fall in love. I liked that it is a love comedy about the covers that people create for themselves.'

New York actress Julia Stiles was selected to play Kat, the 'shrew' of Shakespeare's title. Heath recalled his first meeting with her: 'When we read together, there was an instant spark. We were just firing back at each other. We saw it in our eyes.' For her part, Stiles was equally taken with her unknown Australian co-star. 'Heath is a great actor,' she said during production. 'There is some interesting chemistry between us.' Director Junger was certainly pleased by what he saw on screen. 'They are a tremendously sexy couple because they have that kind of brooding quality, yet underneath you know there's real heart in both of them.

Happy endings. Kat is finally tamed.

They walk a very fine line in portraying distant characters who are, at the same time, charismatic.'

With the cast assembled, shooting began in Tacoma, Washington, with the local Stadium High School doubling as the film's main location. As unlike the run-of-the-mill LA high school as it could be, the old Gothic-style building prompted changes to the movie. Several scenes were redrafted to include aspects of the unusual location, such as the nearby Stadium Bowl (down the hill next to the school, on a cliff overlooking the sea) and surrounding countryside.

This background greatly enhances the scene where Ledger indulges his long-standing love of old song-and-dance movies, played out to 'Can't Take My Eyes Off of You'. 'Between the choreographers and me, we kind of played with it,' remembered Heath. 'We wanted a bit of Gene Kelly and Fred Astaire influence. It was totally choreographed and then I just made it sloppy.'

As well as getting to play Shakespeare (almost), now Heath could indulge his childhood fantasies of being a musical star, too. 'I'm not usually a singer, but I was a singer that day. I felt like a rock star. We went into a studio and put down the track, then we did the whole classic thing that they used to do in the old musicals. They'd play it back over loudspeakers and I did this dance number up and down the staircase, while I was singing the song.'

'I wouldn't have got a look in without having a film out like *10 Things I Hate About You*.' – Heath Ledger

Even with the adjustment to shooting in a foreign country, Ledger found filming over eight weeks in America a little easier than shooting in his homeland. 'In Australia, budget and time constraints tend to be tighter,' he told his old school's website. 'It puts greater pressure on the cast and crew to perform regardless of weather conditions, location problems or whatever. This translates into a different work tempo.'

The movie was released at the end of March 1999, to a much louder fanfare than *Two Hands*. Finally, here was the movie that put Heath Ledger on the Hollywood map. The *Chicago Sun-Times* critic Roger Ebert was impressed by the Australian: 'I liked the sweet, tentative feeling between Ledger and Stiles. He has a scene that brings the whole movie to an enjoyable halt. Trying to win her heart, he waits until she's on the athletic field, and then sings over the PA system, having bribed the school's marching band to accompany him. Those scenes are worth the price of admission.' *Variety* saw the film as appealing to less discerning teens, but singled out that musical scene again: 'At its most promising (as in a sequence where Patrick serenades Kat with help from the marching band and football field sound system), *10 Things* aims for an anything-goes silliness . . . The cast is decent, with Aussie transplant Ledger an assured lead.' *The San Francisco Chronicle*'s Mick La Salle called Stiles and Ledger 'bright and attractive . . . [They] make the most of their scenes together,' while, somewhat surprisingly, independent film magazine *Film Threat* called the movie 'the best teen film of the year'.

Heath relished the Shakespearean origins of his 10 Things I Hate About You *character, Patrick Verona. The film is a modern re-imagining of the Bard's classic play* The Taming of the Shrew.

Heath Ledger was paid a little under $100,000 for his role in *10 Things I Hate About You*. While to him it seemed a huge amount of money, by Hollywood standards it was nothing. But it was just about enough to support the actor in his new digs in New York for the better part of a year. It would be that long before he stepped back in front of a camera again.

'After *10 Things* I had a lot of opportunities to do more teen flicks, but I didn't really want to,' said Heath. 'I was raising my stakes, going for better scripts and better filmmakers. Each time I would get really close and then at the last minute, the rug would be whipped out from under me.' Packaged by the makers of *10 Things* as the next in a seemingly never-ending line of teen idols, Ledger was determined to avoid such a fate. He wanted longevity in his career, to tackle serious parts and work with the best directors on the most interesting projects. He knew that to get stuck – for however short a time – in the teen idol sector would be a huge drawback. He was able to avoid it, but nearly starved while waiting for the right role to come his way. 'I just had to stick with it. I was prepared to go back home and make movies in Australia. Your friends are calling you crazy, and you're like, "I'm not. I promise you. You'll see." I didn't want to get stuck in that rut, [but] I was living off two-minute noodles!'

'After *10 Things* I had a lot of opportunities to do more teen flicks, but I didn't really want to. I was raising my stakes, going for better scripts and better filmmakers.'
– Heath Ledger

He kept himself occupied, indulging his hobbies: playing chess ('I've played since I was a kid,' he told MTV.com, 'I play at least one game a day.' In his early years he regularly beat his father at chess, and some sources claim he was state junior champion at age ten), going for drives in his 1970 Mustang or occasionally taking a trip to Los Angeles - doubling up business meetings with a visit to a friend who worked on a horse ranch in the Hollywood hills, close to the famous Hollywood sign. 'We'd go out there, jump on the horses and ride through the night,' said Heath. It turned out to be a good thing that the young actor had kept his horse-handling skills fresh.

For all his stubbornness, as time wore on Heath became less sure that he was ever going to win a suitable role. 'I would rather do nothing than do something I was unhappy with. I would do a bad job,' he protested. Nonetheless, he was letting his craft get more than a little rusty.

After a year away from the screen, the Australian actor finally found a role he felt he could be proud to play, in a film that could hardly be more American.

The Patriot was developed by screenwriter Robert Rodat and producer Mark Gordon, who'd worked together with Steven Spielberg on *Saving Private Ryan*. Their idea was to feature a human drama with the American War of Independence as a backdrop. 'From the time I was a kid, the American Revolution always fascinated me,' said Rodat. 'I never understood why there wasn't a movie that had captured that.'

The film was soon in development at Columbia, with the producer-director team of Dean Devlin and Roland Emmerich (director of *Independence Day*) at the helm. Hailing from Germany, Emmerich seemed an odd choice for such intrinsically American subject matter. His casting of not one but two Australians in the lead roles seemed positively perverse.

Finding a star name to fill the boots of heroic but troubled main character Benjamin Martin was the first big challenge. 'There are very few people who I think audiences would buy in this role,' said co-producer Mark Gordon. 'When we were developing the screenplay, it was always Mel Gibson that we had in mind. We felt that he was able to play the physicality and the roughness of the character, but at the same time he has enormous humanity and great heart.'

'He told me at one stage, when he was trying to get work in LA, he got down to his last $150. And he used to go to industry functions so he could eat madly and fill his belly.' – Annie Murtagh-Monks

The character of Martin was a challenge even to someone as experienced as Gibson. 'He's tempered by his past, by having children and by remorse for the sins he thinks he has committed during the [French-Indian] war,' explained the actor. 'He's motivated by the fear that he could easily regress, and that his sins and transgressions will come back to haunt him – that he will have to pay a moral debt that will mean losing what he has. His family, his farm, the new life he has built – he just wants to hang on to all of it so hard that it starts slipping through his fingers. Eventually, he finds that he has to either get into the conflict or do nothing and watch as his family is torn apart.'

Due to Martin's initial hesitation and fears about entering the War of Independence, the true patriot of the film is not the father, but his son Gabriel – the role that brought Heath Ledger to the film. 'I thought it would be interesting to have the teacher in this case be the son,' explained screenwriter Rodat. 'Gabriel is a decent, moral guy, and he wears that mantle of principle and responsibility more easily than his father does.'

'There's an assumption that everybody's patriotic, and not everybody is. This movie is called *The Patriot*, but Benjamin Martin is not a patriot. He knows what war is and feels that we should avoid it under all circumstances,' Emmerich noted.

When the possibility of the role in *The Patriot* came up, Heath was ready to work. 'I was hungry at times,' he admitted to *Vanity Fair*. '[*The Patriot*] was my last hope. If I didn't get the part, I was going to go back home. I had nothing. No money. No nothing . . . At one point, I didn't even want to read the script and go in and meet with them. I had come so close to so many great projects that I just had the rub taken out of me.'

Luckily, he did take the time to audition for director Emmerich, but it would prove a memorable occasion for all the wrong reasons. 'I had two scenes to read and was halfway through the second scene and just stopped,' remembered Ledger. 'I said, "I'm sorry, This is shit. I'm wasting your time." I was so [down] in the dumps I just didn't give a shit. I stood up, I shook their hands and walked off down the hall with my tail between my legs. I walked out.'

Thankfully, his odd behaviour didn't count against him. 'It was down to Heath and one other fellow,' said Mel Gibson, strongly implying that Ledger's closest competition for the part was Ryan Phillippe. 'At first Roland wanted me to decide, but I couldn't,' Gibson claimed. 'So I told him that he was the director. He should make the decision, and I would be happy with it. And I was.'

Heath was amazed that he was even considered for the part, after what he saw as his horrendous audition. 'They must have been a little curious about my behaviour, because I ended up getting called back.'

Emmerich saw something in him that was important to the character of Gabriel. 'Heath did blow that first audition,' he confirmed, 'but you felt in the room, when he walked in, that everybody was kind of immediately straightening up and saying, "Who is this guy?" And he has quite an effect on women.'

Gibson too could recognise Ledger's nascent star quality. 'Heath possesses an unlikely combination: he has incredible presence, yet he has no pretensions. He's much more grounded than I was at that age, when it all started happening for me. I think he'll handle it better than I did.'

'He's 21-years-old, but he doesn't feel like a little boy. He feels like a man.'
– Dean Devlin, producer of *The Patriot*

Rodat saw the same attributes in Ledger that Gibson had. 'We didn't want the character of Gabriel to be a boy,' he said. 'We wanted him to be someone stepping from the dry stone of childhood to the slippery rock of adulthood. We wanted him to be straddling that line.'

Devlin admitted it had been a very tricky part to cast. 'We needed someone who could go toe-to-toe with Mel Gibson . . . On the first day of shooting, Heath was a little shaky. But by the second day, he was slugging it out with Mel scene for scene. It was interesting to watch.' Soon the deal was done and Ledger was on board as Gabriel, but the shoot would not be easy.

'While Gabriel is growing up, he hears these fantastic war stories, and it's all very heroic and glorious to him,' said Heath of his character. 'His father knew better, knew how gory it could be. He doesn't want to put his son in that situation. I think all parents and children go through that sort of thing at some point. Gabriel represents the new generation. He believes strongly in the new ideals of the new country, so he defies his father to go to war.'

The role set a big challenge for the still relatively inexperienced young actor. Ledger's character matures from a boy to a man as his youthful patriotism collides with the bloody reality of war. The part required an actor who could convey both Gabriel's boyish enthusiasm and the strength he develops as he matures. His character also narrated the movie via a voiceover of his letters home, and was charged with embodying the spirit of 1776 – as well as personifying the heavy-handed patriotism inherent in the film's title, such as when he's seen solemnly mending a colonial flag. It also demanded an actor who could convincingly pass as Gibson's screen son. 'Heath possesses qualities that link him to Mel, and I think that on screen that really comes off as a very believable father and son relationship,' said producer Devlin. 'If you look at the very early Mel Gibson movies, even when he was very young, he never seemed like a boy. There was something very manly about him, even at a young age. I think that is true about Heath Ledger. He's 21-years-old, but he doesn't feel like a little boy. He feels like a man. I think they share that quality on screen. You feel that there is a weight to the things they have to say about the cause.'

Gibson was equally impressed with his co-star's intensely earnest approach. 'I really like the kid,' he said. 'He is far more mature than his age. He was very measured and very deliberate about his work. I remember what I was like when I was that age. God, I don't think I was capable of some of the more subtle things he did. He was very accurate, precise and subtle in what he did. I think he's got a hell of a future. He's got the right sort of heart and spirit for the whole thing, and he's just going to get better as he goes on.'

Historical epic The Patriot *(2000) provided Heath with his first taste of film-making at the blockbuster level.*

Heath was happy to return the compliment to his mentor and compatriot – after all, if he ever chose to emulate anyone's career, he could have done a lot worse than Gibson's. 'That first day we started shooting, it was weird. I hadn't been in front of a camera for over a year and there I was with Mel Gibson . . . I was very nervous, because he was a guy I always looked up to. He was Mad Max! Working with Mel really opened up a lot inside of me, in terms of discovering how to relax in your working environment, keeping your head clear . . . It's subtextual, how he teaches you. Of course, it all comes down to being willing to be taught.'

Ledger was in awe of Gibson's ability to focus on his work during the take, and

'I was hungry at times. *The Patriot* was my last hope.
If I didn't get the part, I was going to go back home. I had nothing.
No money. No nothing.' – Heath Ledger

Above and right: Heath co-starred with fellow Aussie Mel Gibson in The Patriot.
The role of the idealistic Gabriel was his first in over a year.

Gabriel (Heath) experiences the dark side of the American Revolution.

'He is far more mature than his age. He was very measured and very deliberate about his work. I think he's got a hell of a future, and he's just going to get better as he goes on.' – Mel Gibson

then just as enthusiastically joke and chat between scenes. Fond of puns, an engaging storyteller with a seemingly endless supply of jokes, Gibson kept the mood light – even inviting the Carolina Panthers' cheerleaders to a battlefield set for Roland Emmerich's birthday. It gave Heath a model lesson on how a star should behave on set, something he would find handy in later years when he was top of the bill and had other actors looking up to him.

Production of *The Patriot* began on 7 September 1999, by which time the team had assembled 63 principal actors, almost 100 stuntmen, 400 extras and 400 historical society 're-enactors' to fill out the backgrounds. It was shot at various locations throughout South Carolina, in and around a small community called Rock Hill – which offered a unique block of colonial homes, a living history village and a

Revolutionary War battlefield site – before ending up in the city of Charleston in early December. After taking in several historical plantations, *The Patriot* wrapped production at a manmade marsh near Charleston known as Cypress Gardens, a fully realised swamp created in the late 1920s. There the unit filmed crucial scenes between Ledger and Gibson, over several chilly nights. On the last evening, the cast and crew were rewarded for their perseverance with the sight of a rare lunar eclipse.

Making *The Patriot* had a profound effect on Heath. 'I gained a lot of respect for this country,' he admitted, now realising he was destined to live and work in the US. 'I'd always wondered why Americans were so proud and why they waved their flags so high and sang their songs so loud. It was because they went through hell and back to get this country – and dammit, if I was an American, I'd be proud too.'

'Heath possesses an unlikely combination: he has incredible presence, yet he has no pretensions.' – Mel Gibson

The movie opened to a mixed reception from critics in June 2000. Roger Ebert of the *Chicago Sun-Times* called *The Patriot* 'a cartoon . . . None of it has much to do with the historical reality of the Revolutionary War.' Mick La Salle, in the *San Francisco Chronicle*, singled out Ledger for his 'good job as a young fellow who impulsively joins the war for romantic reasons but grows a sense of purpose', while *Rolling Stone* called him an 'Aussie newcomer [who] has the talent and looks to become a major star'. *The Patriot* also proved to be Ledger's first bona fide blockbuster movie, hitting a total US box office take of over $113 million (compared with *10 Things I Hate About You*'s $38 million).

Heath Ledger's appearance in *10 Things I Hate About You* brought him a teenage fanbase which would follow him from film to film – although he was initially slow in realising it. 'This is all very weird,' he said of the adoration now being directed his way. 'I don't take a lot of this all that seriously.'

Having recently returned home to Perth on a visit, though, he'd become aware of just how extensive his newfound fame had become. 'If I walk on the streets back home, I get recognised. It is a little weird, a little crazy. But it's fine. I don't stress about it. I still enjoy living my own life in my own world with my friends.'

But while he professed not to be worried about the effect on his life, in almost the same breath he admitted his concern about the reality of fame. 'My career's in a weird transition stage right now. When I come home people recognise me. It does frighten me and it's not fun.'

The Patriot, meanwhile, had shown that this new teen idol was capable of drawing upon hidden dramatic depths to play parts that seemed beyond his years.

3. GOLDEN YEARS

'I want to keep the choice to say no.
I'm in control of my life, not anyone in Hollywood.
I only do this because I'm having fun. The day
I stop having fun, I'll just walk away.'
– Heath Ledger

Having spent a year avoiding teen typecasting before *The Patriot*, Heath Ledger was in no mood to repeat the experience of being out of work. Although now 21-years-old, he was aware that movie producers would still trade on his youthful good looks. Such was clearly the case with his next starring role in the medieval comedy adventure romp *A Knight's Tale*. That didn't mean that Ledger was happy about it.

'That was a movie where they put my face up there and put, "He will rock you" on the poster, and if I didn't, or the movie didn't, I was fucked,' said Ledger, who took the pressure to live up to the hype perhaps a little too seriously for his own good.

'They were kind of putting my career in their hands, out of my control. They were determining whether I would work again, and it put this unnecessary pressure on me. It was the first time I'd really been thrown into this position of running the show, and it really is intimidating when it first happens. It's scary. . . If it doesn't work, it's my fault.'

Ledger had a tendency to internalise such pressures. He took his responsibilities to each movie seriously, but simply didn't enjoy the promotional aspects or the idea of being a manufactured movie star, rather than an actor. 'I want to keep the choice to say no,' Ledger insisted. 'I'm in control of my life, not anyone in Hollywood. I only do this because I'm having fun. The day I stop having fun, I'll just walk away. I wasn't going to have fun doing a teen movie again. I don't want to do this for the rest of my life. I don't even want to spend the rest of my youth in this industry. There's so much more I want to discover.'

A Knight's Tale was the directorial debut of Oscar-winning screenwriter Brian Helgeland (*LA Confidential*). The storyline was suggested by one of Chaucer's *Canterbury Tales*, but Helgeland wanted his historical adventure to have a much

He Will Rock You. Heath's breakthrough role in A Knight's Tale *(2001)*
put his 22-year-old face on billboards around the world.

more contemporary feel. 'For a historical movie to work, the audience has to be invited in,' he felt. 'They can get pushed away if overwhelmed by period costumes, obscure speech and antique music.' He wanted his film to contain 'relatable elements. Our goal was to create a seamless bridge between then and now. We wanted to create a period piece that stayed fair to the period, but felt contemporary.'

Helgeland was also concerned, while writing the script, that he was creating a character not many actors may have been capable of playing. 'When I first wrote the part [of William], he had to ride, sing, dance, sword fight and joust,' Helgeland remembered. 'I wondered, "Who am I going to get to play this and also have this kind of self-possession to him?" It's hard to find that in a young person, never mind a young actor.'

It was Amy Pascal, co-producer on the movie and head of Columbia Pictures, who had the answer. As producer of *The Patriot*, she didn't have to wait for that movie to open before earmarking Heath Ledger for the lead in *A Knight's Tale*. 'He's the real thing,' Pascal told *Vanity Fair*, explaining why she signed him solely on the basis of *The Patriot*'s dailies. Ledger won the lead role over many bigger names after a jet-lagged meeting with Helgeland during which he serenaded the director with a didgeridoo ('I must've made something of an impression,' Heath noted dryly), and this time didn't have to suffer the humiliation of an audition – a process he'd already come to fear.

'They were kind of putting my career in their hands, out of my control. They were determining whether I would work again, and it put this unnecessary pressure on me.' – Heath Ledger

'It was the first time I had been offered a movie [without auditioning],' explained Ledger. 'I was like, "Yeah, I don't have to audition, great, just whack me in there." Then it got me super nervous: why, and what was their plan? I had all these conspiracy theories. It was a Columbia picture like *The Patriot* and I thought: "What are they leading me up to?" It got me paranoid.'

Having resisted typecasting as a teen idol, Ledger now feared that Columbia had plans to turn him into some kind of branded action hero figure instead. 'Reading the script, it was obvious to me that it was an ensemble piece. I never remember feeling any pressure during the shooting. The only time I did was when I saw my face on the poster afterwards. You can't help but be intimidated by that.'

As for Helgeland, he was just happy to have found an actor who could carry off the demands of the lead role. 'When Heath smiles, it's Errol Flynn,' he said, summing up the early Ledger's old-fashioned appeal. 'Once every 50 years a guy like that comes along. For his age, Heath has an incredible manliness about him.'

Helgeland's Flynn comparison is a very valid one, especially in the context of *A Knight's Tale*. The movie has much of Flynn's 1938 *The Adventures of Robin Hood* about it, and Ledger had much of his fellow Antipodean's easy charm in his role as William Thatcher.

Director of photography Richard Greatrex, whose other credits included historical dramas *Mrs. Brown* and *Shakespeare in Love*, was convinced of Ledger's

A reluctant studio 'It' boy, Heath was uncomfortable being the focus of the marketing campaign that spearheaded the release of A Knight's Tale.

future stardom. 'I'd shot his screen test for a Miramax film called *Calcio*, which is the Italian word for football. It was about an English football fan who ends up in Sardinia. The film got cancelled at the last minute because Harvey Weinstein [Miramax co-chairman] didn't like Heath. The director and Harvey had quite a disagreement about him, and the thing fell apart only a week before we were to start shooting. I think Harvey must be kicking himself, considering all the buzz about the boy.'

With *A Knight's Tale*, Ledger's salary had now escalated to the point where he was an official member of the $1 million club, and in future could command in excess of that figure for each film. For his part he was looking forward to headlining his own movie, even if the prospect made him nervous. 'It's going to be mentally labouring because it's the first big movie I have the lead in,' Ledger told *Detour* magazine as he prepared for filming. 'I guess I'm a little nervous about driving the bus. Before, I got to sit behind Mel [Gibson] and pat him on the back and go, "Hey, keep driving, you're doing a good job. We're all happy back here. Just make sure we get off this bus safe." Now, I have to step up and sit in the driver's seat.'

The $45 million project was shot in Prague's historic Barrandov Studios in the Czech Republic, allowing for much higher onscreen production values on what was a relatively tight budget. Several giant exterior sets were constructed on site, and the production had the use of the surrounding Czech countryside. Covering an area larger than two American football fields, the sets included medieval London, Rouen in France, and three diverse jousting fields.

'I'm the worst auditioner; really, really bad. I mean, you're being judged and I'm just so aware of it that it consumes me. I can't relax, I'm tied in knots. It's foul. I hate it.'
– Heath Ledger

Ledger found that the surroundings really allowed him to get a handle on his character. The realistic environments constructed in the Prague countryside set a real physical context within which he could explore the background to his role. 'I'm an impostor knight called William Thatcher,' he said. 'My father sends me off to work as a squire for a knight. He dies in a tournament and I jump into his armour and complete the competition. What really appealed to me is not so much that William changes his stars, but what he learns in doing so. He goes for the gold, the nobility and fame, but ultimately discovers that the friends who surround and support him are the real stars in his life. The real nobility is finding your head and your heart.'

Helgeland added: 'Ledger's William is the focus. His is a modern archetypal American story of a self-made person who hurdles social barriers. By the time William is ennobled by royalty, he has already been ennobled in his heart. This is a fairy tale. *A Knight's Tale* is a tribute to anyone who has accomplished something very far-fetched.'

Soon Ledger's lowborn character is passing himself off as the fictitious noble Sir Ulrich von Lichtenstein of faraway Gelderland, in a scam cooked up by him and his friends. Things don't run smoothly, of course. William and his little band of merry men (and women) come across a ruthlessly charismatic champion named Count Adhemar (Rufus Sewell), who is determined to smash the young man's dreams of success.

Ledger discovered that he was in for weeks of playing a physically demanding role. As well as having to wear heavy (albeit fake) armour much of the time, the actor had to learn jousting techniques too. '[That's] another wacky skill that I've picked up,' he said, nonetheless glad to use his horse-riding skills again so soon after *The Patriot*. 'It just seems like I can't get off a horse – I'm on a horse in every bloody movie I've done! I've been riding since I was a kid so the only thing I had to get used to was the lance. Jousting is tame by comparison with Aussie sports,' Ledger noted of his hockey-playing days. 'I got to wrap myself in metal and jump on a horse and charge at some other guy on a horse. It was fun, except for the stuff where I got hit. The lances were quite heavy. The hardest thing was keeping them balanced on a target.'

Once again, despite initial reluctance, he found his inner Gene Kelly. 'I found the dancing scenes in the film much harder to do [than the jousting],' Ledger claimed, modestly asserting, 'I'm not one of nature's most gifted dancers.'

'I don't want to do this for the rest of my life. I don't even want to spend the rest of my youth in this industry. There's so much more I want to discover.' – Heath Ledger

Actor Paul Bettany, in the role of a comically eloquent Geoffrey Chaucer (complete with his own nude scenes), highly praised Ledger's approach to the leading role. 'Heath is a joy to be around . . . [He has] an enormous amount of confidence at a young age. There's a certain grace in being under a lot of pressure. You've got no choice except to be relaxed. You don't have to fight for anything when so many people are putting that much faith in you.'

Despite the pressure of carrying the film, Ledger was able to enjoy the process. 'The set was like a playground for all of us. I not only got to act with an amazing ensemble cast, but I rode horses, sang, danced, did sword fighting, comedy and stunts. [It was] an actor's dream.'

Capturing his desired contemporary feel in the cast and their characters' attitudes, in another inspired move Helgeland scored the film with iconic modern pop songs. The film opened to Queen's 'We Will Rock You', while William and his friends underwent training to War's 'Low Rider'. Bachman-Turner Overdrive's 'Takin' Care of Business' was used to establish William's emergence as a real leader. In the novel dance scene, David Bowie's 'Golden Years' reinforced the idea of love as a kind of magic, whatever the century. 'We aren't trying to sell sequences with pop songs,' said the director. 'We tried to make all the modern touches, particularly the music, very much organic to the movie.'

Despite all the fun of shooting the movie, Heath soon found himself drafted into the serious business of selling it to an audience. 'We filmed in Prague, but I didn't take it too seriously,' he said of making the film, ' . . . we drank and partied, I was often hung-over, it was all a romp. In Prague, it's fifteen cents for about a gallon of beer and it's a beautiful old city, so luckily we had two months where we weren't working. Rufus [Sewell] and I were just exploring the city, but as soon as we started filming, we had to start behaving . . . Then, when we finished, my agent says, "Columbia wants to discuss the promotional campaign." I go, "Eeehh?"'

Heath put his exceptional horse riding skills to good use on the Prague set of A Knight's Tale.

As he soon discovered, he was expected to play a big part in that process. Ledger was summoned to a meeting in the Columbia boardroom with fifteen suits from the marketing department. There he saw the posters with his face front and centre, above the slogan, 'He will rock you'. 'I'm freaking out,' he recalled of his realisation that the film's success or failure rested squarely upon his shoulders. 'They outlined their plan for the release: "We're sending you around America, to twenty states, then twenty countries around the world." I got this two-hour spiel on how they were turning me into Columbia's new "It" boy. I couldn't speak. I left the boardroom, found a bathroom, shut the door, and just started crying.'

Ledger suffered a full-on anxiety attack in the bathroom, as the realisation sank in that it was his face, and his face alone, all over the promotional material. 'I'd been concentrating on how to act,' he said of his Hollywood apprenticeship, 'not how to be a salesman. Agents, publicists, they all say, "Go on *Letterman* and say, 'Hey! I've got a joke!'" When you sit there, honest and nervous, like a normal human being, you get written down as boring and ungrateful.'

He was forced to explain to his agent, Steve Alexander, why he had such trouble with Columbia's plans. 'I tell Steve I can't do it, I don't want my life to be in their hands. I'm not ready to be seen on such a grand scale, I can't act well enough yet. I don't want a career handed to me on a platter: it's too easy. It wouldn't be mine because I haven't earned it. It feels wrong.'

According to Ledger's own account, things took a turn for the worse when Columbia's head honcho intervened: 'I had Amy Pascal on the phone to me: "Listen kid, hear this, your career will be over, you'll never work again, you'll never live again unless you do this for me." I dig Amy now, we've been through a lot of battles and she's cool, but that time was so heavy. In the end I agreed to do part of the promotional tour only, providing they flew my family and Perth friends to America for two weeks.'

It cost Columbia the expense of flying in a total of fourteen friends and family to support Heath on his publicity tour. However, the young actor found himself haunted by the *A Knight's Tale* poster and its advertising slogan, as giant billboards went up all over LA. 'What if I don't rock 'em?' he wondered. 'I pretty much had anxiety attacks about just leaving the house.'

'I don't have to prove anything to anyone. I never have had to and I've never wanted to. I just have fun, and I love what I'm doing.' – Heath Ledger

Ultimately, he must have been gratified by the response of the critics. Jami Bernard in the *New York Post* called *A Knight's Tale* 'charmingly spirited', while Rick Groen in the *Toronto Globe and Mail* reckoned it 'a bouncy pop song of a movie'. For Lou Lumenick in the *New York Post*, it was 'a solidly entertaining popcorn movie'. Even the irascible Roger Ebert, in the *Chicago Sun-Times*, could see the film had 'an innocence and charm that grows on you'. Not all the reviews were positive, though. Bob Longino in the *Atlanta Journal-Constitution* decided *A Knight's Tale* was 'a tale that didn't need to be told . . . so Three-Stooges silly that even the horses look embarrassed'. Heavyweight critic Kenneth Turan in the *Los Angeles Times* maintained that while the film had 'a surprisingly serviceable gimmick', it failed to deliver on it, while Heath looked 'more like a pouty surfer than a pile-driving knight' and his love interest, newcomer Shannyn Sossamon, acted like the 'complete beginner' she was. Glenn Whipp, the *Los Angeles Daily News*' critic, found a couple of scenes funny, but otherwise said it was a 'frustratingly flawed, overlong epic'.

Still, the public, and Ledger's growing fan base, took to the movie well enough. Opening in May 2001 on just under 3,000 screens, the film grossed $16.5 million on its first weekend. It was not a blockbuster, by any means, but it performed steadily, reaching a total US gross of $56 million by the end of its theatrical run in July. The film would do well internationally and on DVD release. Its biggest effect, though, would be on Heath's career: he was now a genuine Hollywood leading man, whether he liked it or not.

Heath Ledger's rise to fame in America had been swift. In the space of under two years he'd gone from being an unknown Australian actor from an obscure TV show to a poster boy for a major studio production. He now had to adjust to the entertainment media's attentions in a way that he just hadn't known before. 'I don't read everything that people write about me: good or bad. I don't like to. I just don't

'I don't want a career handed to me on a platter: it's too easy. It wouldn't be mine because I haven't earned it. It feels wrong.' – Heath Ledger

'You always know when you meet somebody who's going to be a movie star, because they sparkle. And as much as Heath sometimes tried to hide his sparkle, it just came through. It was that boyish, sexy, misunderstood, James Dean thing that we are always looking for. He had it.'
– Amy Pascal, head of Columbia Pictures

Left: *Heath sweats it out in a suit of armour.*
Above: *'Impostor knight' William Thatcher (Heath) prepares to change his stars.*

listen to it or read it and I don't buy into it. It's not worth thinking about.'

But however much he might try, he would find it hard not to think about the press. While he was willing to promote *A Knight's Tale*, Ledger was less than happy to talk about himself. Newfound fame meant that it was unavoidable, however. 'I haven't stopped working until now,' he confirmed, 'so I didn't really have the chance to think about it or let it sink in. Over the last few months I've had to think more about this celebrity thing long and hard. I don't really know how you can prepare yourself for it, though, because you don't know what to expect.'

The least appealing part of the movie process was promoting the finished film. Touring radio and TV stations across the world was a grind that made Ledger antsy. 'The promotional side, the feeling like a product, the being used as a product, being a product – that sucks,' he admitted. 'It frustrates me. People are like, "Well, it's part of the game." You don't have to fully play along with it. You can mould it and sculpt it the way you want it, and if people get shitty about it, it's too bad. Of course, everyone around you professionally, all the studios, want you to go out and do everything [possible].'

As Ledger told the *Dallas Observer*, in a behind-the-scenes account of the press tour, 'I am not getting anything out of this. Where I benefit professionally is purely by people seeing the movie, not by listening to me talk or finding out anything about me. I'm not in a hurry to be a star.'

'I didn't read anything that got written about us, so that helped a lot. I prefer to date older women because they don't try to act older like younger girls, but because they try to act younger.' – Heath Ledger

One other reason he was under scrutiny from the press was his new relationship with fellow thespian Heather Graham. The couple had met in Prague while he was filming *A Knight's Tale* and she was making *From Hell* with Johnny Depp. Ms Graham had also featured in David Lynch's controversial TV series *Twin Peaks*, before starring in movies like *Boogie Nights* and *Lost in Space*. Notable previous relationships had been with troubled British pop star Adam Ant and actor/director Ed Burns.

As with Heath's previous relationships, she was older than him – in this case by nine years. The age difference wasn't as much of an issue for the press as the fact that two Hollywood stars had hooked up. 'It didn't complicate anything personal about the way we felt toward each other,' said Ledger. 'You can't complicate that . . . I didn't read anything that got written about us, so that helped a lot. I prefer to date older women because they don't try to act older like younger girls, but because they try to act younger.'

Speaking of Heather, Heath told *Movieline* magazine, 'She's a beautiful, beautiful girl. We make each other laugh. She's so funny, that's the key. It's fun. It's a good relationship and a very truthful one.'

This was the first time Ledger became aware of photographers going out of their way to capture shots of him away from the movie set, something that would become a serious problem for him later in his career. 'Most of the time you don't

Heath embarked upon his first serious Hollywood romance with actress Heather Graham, nine years his senior. The couple met in Prague while Heath was filming A Knight's Tale.

even know that they're there,' he said of the paparazzi's growing interest. 'That's the scary thing. The whole process of being followed around by photographers, on your own or when you are with somebody, is really strange and invading. I'm still working it all out, so I don't let it bother me. I really try and find humour in it all. It really is funny if you think about it.'

However, Heath had risen from obscurity so fast that he wasn't really prepared for the consequences. 'The past year has just been mad for me,' he said in 2001. 'I haven't really had a chance to let the fame thing sink in or ask questions about it all.'

Back home in Australia, with the double whammy of *The Patriot* and *A Knight's Tale*, Heath's family found themselves repeatedly pursued by the press for information about his childhood and his personal likes and dislikes. 'All this has been strange for my family, but interesting as well because they've been experiencing similar little changes like people calling them up who they haven't seen in twenty years and the press calling them . . . If anything you wish that if one place wasn't to change it would be your hometown, but I was back there recently and they were documenting every meal I had every day! It was in the newspaper that I ate fettuccini on Tuesday: that's front page news in Perth!'

'I got this two-hour spiel on how they were turning me into Columbia's new "It" boy. I couldn't speak. I left the boardroom, found a bathroom, shut the door, and just started crying.' – Heath Ledger

All the fuss gave Ledger a new perspective on just what – and who – was important to him. 'I tend to detach myself and realise that my life is my five best friends and my twenty friends beyond that and my family. All of a sudden over the past few months there are these people around you, these "associates" and beyond that there's the whole [media] world. It's curious.'

Despite all the press interest, Ledger was determined to do his utmost to keep his private life just that. 'A relationship isn't a professional thing,' he said of his time with Heather Graham, a union that would ultimately last a little over nine months.

When the couple separated in June 2001 – after Heath had completed work on *The Four Feathers* and the two of them had endured their every move being scrutinised during a trip to Australia – Ms Graham was philosophical about the break-up. 'It's hard to go out with someone you really like, it's way more scary,' she said. 'I was afraid to put myself on the line. I would always try to go out with someone who liked me more than I liked them. That way if they hurt you, you say, "Oh I was never really into them." I wanted them to pursue me so that I didn't have to worry about getting rejected.'

Heath described the media frenzy surrounding Heather and him as 'a bit of a circus', but he was determined to deal with it on his own terms. 'I can't let [the press] influence my decisions on who I see. That would be unfair. I think there is a certain breed of person who gets off on the fact that they're dating someone who's famous, and they like to promote themselves. I've tried to keep it private. I am still not telling people about it. I'm promoting a movie, not my personal life, nor

After his first taste of recognition, Heath claimed that fame had not changed him.
'It just changes everyone else.'

myself.' Fame, he insisted, had not changed him. 'It just changes everyone else.'

Now established as a rising leading man, Heath Ledger had more choice but also faced greater difficulty in making his choices. He'd been associated with various parts in the months between when *The Patriot* wrapped, in January 2000, and shooting *A Knight's Tale* that following summer, none of which came to fruition. Previously, he'd lost out on one of the central leading parts in aliens-in-US-high-school TV series *Roswell*, which began airing at the end of 1999. Executive producer (and ex-*Star Trek: The Next Generation* star) Jonathan Frakes admitted, 'We could have had Heath Ledger. We tested him for Jason Behr's part [in *Roswell*], but Fox refused to take him because of *Roar!* Because *Roar!* bombed, they tested him, but didn't hire him.'

There was also a much bigger prize that he'd personally declined: the title role of *Spider-Man* in the 2002 summer blockbuster hit. Among those being considered for the star-making role were Freddie Prinze Jr, Jude Law, Tobey Maguire (who would win the part) and Leonardo DiCaprio.

'I'm a rebel in Hollywood,' Ledger claimed of his refusal to follow career advice. 'People kept telling me I had to do big popcorn movies, they kept talking about "opportunities". I refused to put on tights and play a superhero. I don't want to be a "mega-dude", there's too much baggage that goes along with those kinds of roles.' And besides, 'I just don't care for comics. It would have been stealing someone else's dream. They offered me ridiculous amounts of money to make franchise movies, *Spider-Man* to James Bond.'

'I said, "Heath, you could die." We had just done the scene the day before in which another character says, "I will die if it's God's will." So Heath said to me, "Shekhar, I will die if it's God's will."' – Shekhar Kapur

But these comments were also informed by Heath's low opinion of himself and his abilities. 'I didn't feel like I deserved it,' he lamented. 'I didn't really know how to act properly. I started to feel like a bottle of Coke. There was a whole marketing scheme to turn me into a very popular bottle. Coke tastes like shit, but there's posters everywhere so people will buy it. I felt like I tasted like shit, and I was being bought for no reason.'

But apart from his worries about typecasting or becoming a Hollywood 'product', Ledger had his own criteria about what attracted him to a project. 'I want to read a really great script. I get excited when I read really great work. Therefore, I don't think I would be happy doing anything I wasn't in love with. I just would rather not. I've got other things I can do.'

In committing to *The Four Feathers* (a remake of the acclaimed and much loved 1939 version, based on the classic 1901 A. E. W. Mason novel) as his next film, Ledger was looking to recapture something of the kudos of *The Patriot*. It was the young actor's hope that he might find recognition in serious dramatic roles, rather than taking the easy route of popcorn superhero movies.

Ledger had been approached by director Shekhar Kapur, who'd previously

Heath as Harry Faversham in Shekhar Kapur's The Four Feathers *(2002).*
The film was Ledger's first significant box-office failure.

made the historical epic *Elizabeth*, while shooting *A Knight's Tale* in Prague. 'He called me up and said, "Do you want to come down and audition?"' the actor recalled, 'so I went down and they really put me through a ringer.'

Ledger's ability to handle the audition process had not improved since *The Patriot*. Having scored the lead in *A Knight's Tale* without an audition, he was rusty in the technique of impressing directors and executives. 'It was fucking torturous,' he said of the process. 'Basically, I was improvising for eight hours. [Kapur would] sit me down, roll the camera, and he'd ask me to play Abou, who was Djimon Hounsou's character. [I'd] sit there and talk to Shekhar, who'd play my character. He'd roll camera and be like, "Talk to me about destiny," and at that point I'd read the script like twice. I had no idea what I was doing.'

Given Ledger's dislike of the audition process, it's a wonder he progressed as far as he did as a young actor in Hollywood. 'I get bored in auditions. I hate them,' he admitted. 'It's the most awkward position you can be in. You walk into a room, and you're asked to pour yourself into this piece of material knowing that you're not performing for anyone. You're being tested, you're being judged and you're being watched. It's just a very insecure, vulnerable position to be in.'

'The Four Feathers **was a tough project, it was extremely tough. But that was the exciting thing about it. It was a challenge. And I really liked walking into something like that with fear. There was this fear, just bubbling up in my gut.' – Heath Ledger**

Ledger played straight-arrow Harry Faversham, a young British soldier whose fear of battle leads him to resign his army post days before he's due to fight in the 1884 Sudanese war, in aid of General Gordon of Khartoum. After receiving four feathers (a symbol of cowardice) from his three closest friends and his patriotic girlfriend (Kate Hudson), Harry decides to go to Africa after all, where – disguised as an Arab – he fights to regain his honour, aided by local farmer Abou Fatma (Djimon Hounsou).

It's a classic tale, but it may have seemed out of kilter with the expectations of modern movie audiences. In fact, the movie fell into all the historical-dramatic traps that director Brian Helgeland had gone to great lengths to avoid in *A Knight's Tale*. As a result, the film failed to connect with the young audience that might be expected to attend a movie starring young actors like Ledger and Hudson.

Facing the physical demands of the film meant Ledger had to get in shape. 'Djimon dragged me into the gym, but he kind of gave up half way. I was struggling and he was lifting weights with one arm, so he said, "Forget about it, kid." We did horse riding training, military weapon training, learning how to stand in the posture of the soldier, marching as a soldier, and ballroom dancing. It was kind of refreshing to finally get out there and scream and beat people up and jump on horses.' Echoing his schooldays, Ledger noted, 'The military stuff was boring. You're just standing there like a twig. I enjoyed the dancing. That was fun.'

Director Kapur saw an immediate personal connection to the material. 'I was angered by the previous movies [of the novel], because of where I come from,' said Kapur, whose native India was under British rule from 1858 to 1947. 'They just did

Set during the 1884 Sudanese War, The Four Feathers *required four months of intensive shooting on location in the Moroccan desert.*

not question colonisation. If you look at the state of the world today, you can trace it back to one cause: colonisation.'

The movie was shooting in Morocco, an Islamic nation, during September 2001, when New York was attacked by fundamentalist Muslim terrorists. It was a development that couldn't help but be reflected in the film's subtext. 'Though it's fiction, it's based on the first jihad against a European or a white nation,' noted Kapur. 'All the other versions were about a man who had to go out and prove he wasn't a coward, but [in my version] to question and to doubt and not be suppressed by the morality of your peers is the real act of courage. It's easier to do your duty than question your duty. I wish I had known what would happen in Iraq. I would have gone much further.'

Ledger had been very keen on winning the central role in *The Four Feathers*: ' . . . [it was] just the character. His journey is so epic and he really starts at one place and ends in another . . . I found him to be courageous because he was standing up for what he believed in, against the systematic and regimental lifestyle that he has been spoon-fed his whole life. There was a hell of a lot of subtext to be added. I knew Shekhar would be more than able to provide me with that.'

'I generally don't give a fuck what people think. I've seen it, I like it. I'm proud of it and that's really it. My job's kind of over from this point on, there's nothing more I can do.' – Heath Ledger on the critical reception of *The Four Feathers*

For Ledger, the moral dilemma was the attraction. 'It was the material I responded to. We made *The Four Feathers* in Morocco, and I had a beard and long hair and six different wigs. I was always in make-up. It isn't conscious on my part to do period pieces.'

Or indeed to make films featuring horses – but once again, he found himself drawing on his equestrian skills. 'We had one sequence where I get shot off my horse. I stand up and look behind me and there are about a hundred horses heading towards me,' he recalled. 'There is one horse with no-one in the saddle and as they come towards me I have to run, grab the saddle, bounce off the ground and onto the horse . . . Then in the next part of the sequence in the battle, [I was] galloping and jumping off the horse and onto a guy's back. I got a real kick out of that.'

He insisted on doing the stunt himself. 'Heath came to me and said, "I think I'm going to jump,"' Kapur said. 'I said, "Heath, you could die." We had just done the scene the day before in which another character says, "I will die if it's God's will." So Heath said to me, "Shekhar, I will die if it's God's will."' The sequence became one of the film's standout scenes, but Kapur was subsequently informed by the studio that if he ever again allowed an actor to put themselves in such physical danger, the director's Hollywood career would – in no uncertain terms – be over.

Despite all the physical training, Ledger was finding that the best way to uncover his character was to talk him through with the director and the other cast members. 'Physically there was no way to prepare. We did horse training, firing

Dead Man Walking. Heath's supporting role as suicidal prison guard Sonny in harrowing death row drama
Monster's Ball *(2001) proved that he was capable of giving performances of unnerving depth.*

'Heath really went through a period of time where he wasn't "the guy". He was hard to
get on the proverbial list. Then he decided he was going to build his career back up
the way he wanted it to be. He wanted to play characters that he could disappear into.
I think that started with *Monster's Ball*.' – Steve Alexander

weapons and learning how to walk and talk, the posture of the soldier of that era.
The rest was just talking. We spent four weeks around a table, eight hours a day,
just discussing the movie and creating a brain for each of our characters.'

As he gained more experience in front of the camera, and then further leading
roles, his approach to acting was developing. Having had no training, Ledger
developed his own unique version of method acting. He had begun to internalise
his characters, following a period of research, so that he could 'become' them.

When *The Four Feathers* was released, the film was a box-office disaster. Despite the teen-friendly cast, the concept of the movie was a hard sell to modern audiences. *The Four Feathers* had its North American premiere at the Toronto Film Festival in September 2002, and made its European debut as the closing film at the 29th Flanders International Film Festival on 19 October. Following the Toronto screening, Roger Ebert damned the film in the *Chicago Sun-Times*: 'The problem with *The Four Feathers* is that the characters are so feckless, the coincidences so blatant and the movie so innocent of any doubts about the "White Man's Burden" that Kipling could have written it. Ledger, Hudson and Wes Bentley seem to be playing dress-up.' *Variety* dubbed the movie 'a dull rendition of the old warhorse,' and noted that the 'performances are uniformly undistinguished, with Ledger appearing rugged and long-suffering, but nothing more.' *Rolling Stone* conceded that 'Ledger gives his all', but the film in general was 'weighed down with bogus profundities'.

'Monster's Ball was the first time I felt like I had to do something about it; and what I had to do was essentially nothing. At the time, I just boiled it down, took off the shine, and destroyed it a little bit.' – Heath Ledger

Audiences stayed away. An opening weekend take of just $6 million climbed to a cumulative US total box office of just $18 million, far short of the film's estimated $80 million production budget. *The Four Feathers* was a flop by any standards, the first for Ledger as a leading man. 'The film was cast with teenage idols,' Kapur said. 'It was marketed toward teenagers, but to me it was not a teen film. I think it should have been marketed as a film trying to interpret the contemporary world situation in a historical context.'

Movie industry reporter Jeffrey Wells expressed the more conventional wisdom, on his *Hollywood Elsewhere* blogsite: 'The bottom line is that [Ledger] didn't pull in his young-girl fans, the presumed core supporters of romantic dramas, on the first weekend, and there's no way this helps the guy. His reputation as a hot, ascending movie star with a loyal female fan base is clearly being re-evaluated.'

Ledger had a forthright response to the failure of *The Four Feathers*. 'I generally don't give a fuck what people think. I've seen it, I like it. I'm proud of it and that's really it. My job's kind of over from this point on, there's nothing more I can do.'

Despite the failure of the movie, he was still seen as a rising star within the industry. In 2001, its year of release, he'd won a ShoWest Award for the Male Star of Tomorrow, voted by theatre owners on the basis of his performances in *The Patriot* and *A Knight's Tale*. Responding to the award, Ledger said, 'Oh jeez, it's a little overwhelming. At least they have confidence in my future; that's a good thing.'

Although it was released earlier, Ledger's involvement in *Monster's Ball* came after he'd completed *The Four Feathers*. Like his casting in *10 Things I Hate About You*, it was a last-minute decision. 'Wes [Bentley, Ledger's *The Four Feathers* co-star] was cast in *Monster's Ball* while we were shooting *The Four Feathers* in London,' explained Ledger. 'He had some family issues and had to get back home, so he brought it to me and said, "It's a really good script." I did it for those reasons: great people, cool script.'

It was far from a starring role, but it allowed Ledger to stretch his legs, dramatically speaking. 'I guess I feel a lot more comfortable on a smaller set. It keeps you alive during a smaller movie and smaller roles; there's less pressure. The whole movie was shot in four weeks; my work was over in two days. It's fun to be able to walk in and out, and not have the pressures of creating a huge arc for your character or carrying the movie.'

Monster's Ball starred Halle Berry (who eventually won the Best Actress Oscar for her role) as Leticia, who falls in love with the racist, white prison guard Hank (Billy Bob Thornton) who executed her husband (rap music star Sean Combs, aka Puff Daddy/P. Diddy), although neither of them knows of their connection. Ledger was Hank's suicidal son, Sonny. *Monster's Ball* was filmed in the late spring and summer of 2001, in and around New Orleans and at the notorious Louisiana State Penitentiary at Angola (also know as 'the Farm').

'I couldn't bring myself to call him Puffy because I knew I would laugh,' said Ledger of his rapper co-star. 'We all called him Sean. It was very Pythonesque on set, great fun. It was a pleasure to get up and go to work every day. It was like being at kindergarten.'

Given the gravitas of the film and his small role within it, Ledger seemed to have made a conscious decision to throw off the burden of carrying a big movie like *The Four Feathers*. On *Monster's Ball*, he was out to have fun, not to impress anyone. As a result, he turned in one of his finest and most telling performances. 'I'm just showing up and acting,' he said of his participation. 'A big-budget job doesn't really differ from a low-budget movie like *Monster's Ball*. No amount of money can change what I do between them saying "action" and "cut". You can just go in there and pretty much do what the fuck you want.'

'Over the last few months I've had to think about this celebrity thing long and hard. I don't really know how you can prepare yourself for it though, because you don't know what to expect.' – Heath Ledger

His seemingly breezy approach to the role didn't tell the whole story. However small it was, he was still going to give it his all. 'At this time of my life I just need things that I can sink my teeth into,' he said. 'I want to experience things and learn, and that's the only way to do it. You have to put yourself out there in positions of vulnerability and test yourself, and that's what I'm doing. It's because I'm not a very happy person, but in the future, you will see me smile a bit.'

This admission of not being 'a very happy person' was partly tongue-in-cheek, but behind it lay some elements of truth. (He desperately needed a prestigious breakthrough film, but must have known in his heart that *The Four Feathers* would not be it; he was professionally frustrated with Hollywood; his relationship with Heather Graham had recently ended.) The reality of professional life in Hollywood for an actor had fallen short of Ledger's hopes and aspirations. The 'business' part of 'show business' seemed to dominate, and he'd been expending as much energy on resisting being packaged as a commodity as he had in creating his screen characters. It was frustrating for an actor who felt he was learning with each role he tackled, and that he could offer much more than swinging about New York in a Spider-Man outfit.

'I wanted to take the "blond" out of my career,' he admitted, 'kill the direction it was going. I was like, "Well, how am I gonna make this a career I would like to have?" If no audiences came, "Good. That's gonna help me out."' This self-destructive streak would become more pronounced, but it was not detected in Ledger by any of the filmmakers he worked with early on.

After the release of *The Four Feathers*, Ledger felt he'd succeeded in his mission to destroy himself. Now he could begin rebuilding. 'I got to the point where it worked: Nobody wanted to work with me,' the actor claimed. 'I'd finally – whether consciously or unconsciously – perfectly sabotaged any studio interest in working with me.'

'Why do I act? We need to work to eat. I don't live to work, I work to live. This happens to be something that I love to do. I get a million things out of it, but money is about the most important one.' – Heath Ledger

However, his small but powerful role as the disturbed, suicidal son in *Monster's Ball* was to sow the seeds for two of Ledger's all-time great screen performances. Novelist Larry McMurtry, who wrote the screenplay of *Brokeback Mountain*, saw the movie and concluded, 'That's Ennis,' referring to one of his own main characters. Similarly, Luke Davies, who co-wrote the script of *Candy*, convinced himself, 'That's Dan.'

The Order, the film that reunited Heath Ledger and Brian Helgeland, director of *A Knight's Tale*, was a strange and troubled production.

Helgeland had come across the term 'Sin Eater' almost a decade before, describing a person who absorbed the sins of the dying, thereby absolving them. 'The Sin Eater originated during medieval times when the Catholic Church was extremely powerful,' the writer-director explained. 'If you were dying and had been ex-communicated and couldn't receive last rites, they would send for a Sin Eater, whom they believed would absolve the sins of that person. He would take the sins right into his soul.'

Helgeland saw it as the basis of a horror movie along the lines of mid-1970s classic *The Exorcist*. Having written the script and coming close to pre-production, his attention turned to casting.

He didn't look too far afield, re-hiring Ledger, Shannyn Sossamon and Mark Addy (all from *A Knight's Tale*) for the new movie, made under the title *The Sin Eater* but released in the US as *The Order*. 'I am often asked why I re-teamed with this group,' Helgeland said. 'I always reply that it is for the same reason I go home to the same family for the holidays.'

For his part, Ledger was happy to return to the safety of a familiar team. 'We all feel the same way,' he spoke for the trio of reunited actors. 'We embrace any opportunity to be with Brian, and with each other.'

According to Helgeland, the $35 million supernatural thriller was intended to contain 'a romanticism that horror movies in the last twenty years have lost. It's probably more like *Rosemary's Baby* than anything.' It would star Ledger as Alex, a conflicted priest who fears modernisation within his church. Sossamon was cast as an artist with whom Ledger's priest shares a turbulent past, while Addy played Thomas, the priest's best friend and something of an amateur detective. (German actor Benno Fürmann played the title role of the Sin Eater, an immortal sated with his absorbed experience of evil.) The central trio investigate the myth of the Sin Eater, and find that the character has an effect on each of them.

Principal photography for *The Order* took place in Rome, where the production had failed to secure co-operation from the Vatican, which nonetheless made no attempt to obstruct it. The movie's cast were instructed by religious experts on the ritual elements of their roles, including Latin catechisms, wearing the vestments correctly, priestly deportment and the conducting of exorcisms.

The entire movie was shot in Italy, ranging from Roman locations the Palazzo Taverna (which provided the interior of the film's mansion), Villa

Alex (Heath) is a young priest suffering a crisis of faith in Brian Helgeland's supernatural thriller The Order *(2003).*

Adriana and Villa Aldobrandini to Naples and Caserta in southern Italy, where the Caserta Royal Palace (previously seen in *Star Wars Episode I: The Phantom Menace*) doubled for the Vatican interiors. Returning to Rome, the interior scenes were shot at the famous Cinecitta Studios. While intricate planning went into shooting the film, director Helgeland had to admit that a lively city like Rome had its problems. 'I've heard it said by directors that in Prague, where we did *A Knight's Tale*, you make the film you want to make. But in Rome, you make the film Rome wants you to make. Sometimes, Rome knew best.'

The Order was plagued by both minor and major problems. Thieves walked into the film's production offices one morning and stole around $100,000 at gunpoint, only yards from the soundstage where the cast and crew were filming. 'It's the last thing you expect to happen,' Helgeland said, understating the case somewhat, 'but it made lunch exciting.'

The special effects proved to be another headache. Originally intended for release in January 2003, the film was postponed after test audiences laughed out loud at scenes representing sin flying out of the human body. According to *Entertainment Weekly*, test audiences thought the escaping sins looked more like giant squid or calamari. As a result, the effects work by the UK's Mill Film (who had worked on *Gladiator*) was deemed unusable, and Helgeland hired Santa Monica effects house the Asylum to re-do them.

'At this time of my life I just need things that I can sink my teeth into. You have to put yourself out there in positions of vulnerability and test yourself, and that's what I'm doing.' – Heath Ledger

Eventually released in September 2003, *The Order* was not welcomed by critics (partly because it was not screened to them in advance, usually a bad sign). Stephen Holden in the *New York Times* called *The Order* 'a movie so entranced by its own bogus solemnity that most of what passes for conversation is language warped into the heavy-breathing pontification of prophecy delivered in thudding Charlton Heston-style cadences'. Wesley Morris in the *Boston Globe* merely summed it up as 'a stupendous bore'. The film slowly crawled to a total US box office take of just $7.6 million, very poor against a production budget of $38 million. With *The Order*, Heath Ledger had suffered his second big Hollywood flop, after *The Four Feathers*.

Heath Ledger's solution to his professional and personal travails was to return home to Australia and reconnect with his roots by making a film about a homegrown legend. 'I'm just over it,' he said of Hollywood at the time. 'I just want to come home. I've put in the hard yards.' Based upon fact and legend relating to Australia's own Robin Hood figure, *Ned Kelly* would star Ledger in the title role, a wrongfully imprisoned bushranger in the 1870s who fights for the community against British colonial domination. It would also reunite him with Gregor Jordan, the director who'd launched his screen career with *Two Hands*.

'I've looked up to him since I was a kid,' said Ledger of the legendary Kelly. 'I remember thinking when I was small that I'd love to play him. He represents a lot to me: dignity, especially, and sticking by your family and mates.' He wasn't concerned about playing a character who might be seen as an antihero. 'I'm totally on Ned's side,' he claimed. 'I'm like, "fuck the cops," because what they did to him was terrible and he had just cause to stand up against them.'

In many ways, the film was the Australian version of *The Patriot*, but this time Ledger had graduated to playing the Mel Gibson role of the rebel doing battle with unjust authority. The story had been filmed previously for a badly received 1970 version with Mick Jagger in the central role. For the more definitive version, the leading man cut his asking price considerably from the heady days of his $1 million pay packet for *A Knight's Tale*, agreeing to do the movie for the lowball sum of $60,000. Recognising that it had to be a low-budget movie, Heath was determined to get back to his roots and to work with Jordan again. 'Gregor is my best mate,' declared Ledger. 'There's an easy way of making films, and for me that's by working with your friends.'

'The only way I was prepared to make the movie was with Heath,' concurred Jordan. 'The casting of Ned, a real person, is essential for this film. You need someone who is the right age, physically tall, strong and charismatic. I also felt he should be Australian. So when you add those qualities together, there is really only one person to play the role.'

Jordan had followed the ups and downs of Ledger's Hollywood career. 'Heath made this ballsy choice that he wanted to be an actor, not a star,' the director recognised. 'He'd rather be Sean Penn or Johnny Depp, not Tom Cruise or Brad Pitt. It could have backfired badly, because so many people were waiting to say, "Omigod, look at the roles he's trying to do," when he couldn't pull them off. But Heath did, and I'm proud of him. I've known him since [he was] eighteen, and Heath's always had an old soul.'

Like his favourite director, Ledger had immediately responded to the material: 'I loved how passionate Ned was, and I was excited at the thought of giving life to the legend. Gregor and I had been looking for another project to do together for a while. I thought, "Let's go for it."'

The situation was very different from that on *Two Hands*. Now Ledger was an international star, his coming on board immediately raised the profile of the production. The screenplay, which had attracted both Jordan and Ledger, was kicked back to the writer for revisions, as the original version assumed too much prior knowledge for an international audience.

'There's an easy way of making films, and for me that's by working with your friends.' – Heath Ledger

The association of Ledger with the movie also affected the casting of other members of the Kelly gang. Jordan sought actors to play the other three 'who were all very young – I wanted to cast young lads.' The search for actors in the 18-to-22 age range (rather than mid-twenties and upward, reflecting the genuine ages of the gang) began in Ireland because, as executive producer Tim White explained, 'Ned was as much Irish as he was Australian, so Gregor was keen to go to Dublin to meet with young actors.'

The process brought nineteen-year-old Laurence Kinlan (*Angela's Ashes*) to the film as sensitive Dan Kelly, Ned's little brother. Twenty-year-old Liverpudlian Philip Barantini (*Band of Brothers*) became Kelly gang member Steve Hart, while Jordan also set up a meeting with *Lord of the Rings* star Orlando Bloom in Los Angeles. Bloom was aware of the project, but unaware of the history of Ned Kelly. As he said, 'I thought it was about a bunch of guys shooting guns and riding horses, making havoc wherever they went, until I discovered they were unjustly persecuted and were fighting for freedom and for justice.' Bloom looked at various roles before settling on Joe Byrne because, 'he was Ned's right hand man, his first lieutenant. Joe would live or die for the loyalty of his friends, especially Ned. He would go to hell and back, and that is what he does.'

A couple of other star names were attached to the project. The part of Superintendent Francis Hare went to Oscar-winning Australian actor Geoffrey Rush, while rising Australian actress Naomi Watts signed on to play Julia Cook, Kelly's gentrified, married, English lover. As the rising actress reflected, 'Having grown up in Australia, I know the Kelly Gang is a very important story from our history. I also wanted to work with Gregor and with Heath. After being away [from Australia] for some time, it was wonderful to come back and work on an Australian story.'

Before he started shooting on *Ned Kelly*, Heath was rumoured to have been stepping out with Kirsten Dunst (who played the main squeeze of Spider-Man, the blockbuster role Ledger had missed out on). The pair had been spotted in July 2002, buying perfume and holding hands in Beverly Hill's Saks Fifth Avenue store. (Dunst bought some Printemps Paris scent, reportedly causing Ledger to exclaim, 'It smells like the city of Paree in the springtime. Let's go there!')

'Heath made this ballsy choice that he wanted to be an actor, not a star. He'd rather be Sean Penn or Johnny Depp, not Tom Cruise or Brad Pitt. I'm proud of him. I've known him since he was eighteen, and Heath's always had an old soul.'
– Gregor Jordan

But Ms Watts too was clearly taken with the film's young leading man. 'From day one on set, I was really impressed with Heath. He is both a movie star and an actor. There is always something going on behind his eyes – intelligence, warmth, or sadness.' Before long the pair would become a couple, despite Naomi being eleven years older than Heath.

Ledger wanted to change his appearance dramatically for the film. 'Nobody ever recognises me. In one movie I have brown hair, then blond hair, straight hair, curly hair, now a shaved head,' he said. 'I shaved it for a couple of scenes where Ned gets out of jail.' In order to look as much as possible like the film's antihero, he contacted Oscar-winning make-up and hair designer Jenny Shircore and convinced her to join the project. 'The first person I called was Jenny, who is an absolute genius. Because Ned's look – the beard in particular – is so important for this movie, I did not want to do it without her.'

With Ms Shircore's collaboration, four distinct looks were developed. Depending on what stage of Ned's life was being depicted, up to four hours at a time in the make-up chair were required of the actor. 'Jenny gave me a wonderful mask to hide behind. That in turn gave me the confidence to believe I was the character I was playing. Without that, I really could not have done the work.'

Ledger would use the passive time in the make-up chair to sink himself deep into Kelly's character. He also insisted on bringing in supervising dialect coach Gerry Grennell, who, like so many on the project, was eager to join up. 'Being Irish, I knew

'I don't know what my goals are. I don't know if I want to do it for the rest of my life.
I've never been someone to do one thing. I don't know if I could do just one thing.'
– Heath Ledger

Ned (Heath) and Joseph (Orlando Bloom) live their lives on the run in historical biopic Ned Kelly *(2003),
a portrait of Australia's most notorious outlaw.*

the Ned Kelly story well,' Grennell noted. As Ledger acknowledged, 'Gerry gave a lot of colour and life to my accent. He was able to put me in a real comfort zone where I was able to forget about the accent and perform the story.' It was a new step for Ledger, who'd previously adopted a rather cavalier attitude toward accents.

The actor was also especially struck by a photograph 'of Ned two days before he was hanged. I looked into that portrait and it's all in his eyes; he is very dignified and very proud.'

Production on *Ned Kelly* began on location in rural Victoria, with the assistance of the Melbourne Film Office. 'The whole film was shot within an hour's drive of Melbourne,' noted Jordan. Ledger found himself back in armour for the first time since *A Knight's Tale* – although this time he opted to wear the kind of genuine steel armour that earned Kelly the legendary title 'the Iron Man', and not a movie fake fibreglass version (which was kept as a back-up). 'I needed to know what it felt like to try and walk, manoeuvre, and see with the armour on,' explained Heath of his method. 'They had to make special chairs for us so we could rest between takes, and it took four people with tools to get it on, but I wanted to feel exactly what Ned felt when he stepped out at Glenrowan [the site of a fateful confrontation with the authorities].'

> **'From day one on set, I was really impressed with Heath.**
> **He is both a movie star and an actor. There is always something going on behind**
> **his eyes – intelligence, warmth, or sadness.' – Naomi Watts**

'Shooting many of the scenes was fairly eerie because we were capturing a piece of time,' said Ledger. 'Shooting the Glenrowan sequence – when we stepped out into the rain with our armour on and dozens of policemen were firing metal pellets at us, it felt like we were there that night in June 1880. I realised how crazy the Gang must have been to do it – and that there must have been a real fire in their bellies, that they were fighting for something.'

After filming the intensely emotional scenes inside the Glenrowan Inn, Ledger announced, 'Now I really feel like Ned.' Jordan confided that he found these scenes 'probably the hardest to direct'.

'Ned certainly is going to be carried around in my heart and my mind for some time. He's definitely given me the courage to stand up for, and be true to, what I believe in,' announced Heath. With every new role he was heading deeper into method acting, adopting elements of the character into his own personality. It was obviously a positive process if, as he claimed, he was able to gain courage and self-belief from Ned Kelly. But it might be more disturbing if a darker role was to begin to inform his real-life personality.

As *Ned Kelly* wrapped, Ledger expressed greater satisfaction with his work in it than in his previous two Hollywood movies. 'The whole experience was amazing,' he acclaimed. 'It was such an honour to do this film. [The role of Ned was] something I could really sink my teeth into, a tough rogue.'

Ned Kelly was initially released in the UK in September 2003, pre-empting a later release in the US. Peter Bradshaw in the *Guardian* called it 'sentimentalised but watchable', while singling out Ledger's Kelly as 'a beardless youth who morphs into a ferocious, devious natural leader of men with a chin-in-chest-out strut and a taste for bombastic autobiography'.

Eventually released Stateside in April 2004, Mick La Salle of the *San Francisco Chronicle* dubbed the movie as 'intelligent and well-made as far as action films go, with some effectively staged shoot-outs and with Heath Ledger lending his big-slab-of-a-guy magnetism to the title role'. However, he saw cultural problems with the movie in the US. 'There's something in *Ned Kelly* that's lost in the translation from Australia to America. That Ned had a grievance is undeniable, but to get swept up by the hagiographic treatment, one might really need to be Australian.' He saw Ledger's title character as 'good-looking and earnest, but stiff and not complex'.

The *Hollywood Reporter* was blunt about the star's career status: 'Australian actor Heath Ledger is still chasing a hit. A fixture on magazine covers and drawing all kinds of heat, he's yet to go over the top at the box office.' However, the magazine felt *Ned Kelly* was a better film than either *The Four Feathers* or *A Knight's Tale*, stirring 'together all of the best conventions of the Hollywood Western – gunfights, horseback chases, bank robberies, compromised honour, loyalty and betrayal – while maintaining the story's Australian qualities. The presence of Ledger and the film's high-profile subject almost guarantee strong box-office locally [in Australia].' Again, there was a feeling that, despite the back-up presence of Orlando Bloom and Naomi Watts, *Ned Kelly* would just not travel – although the paper was ultimately positive about the movie itself: 'Held together by Ledger's earthy charisma and Jordan's vigorous mix of action and character, *Ned Kelly* is a striking, stately and ultimately deeply moving experience.'

'People try to make it challenging for us by assuming and creating stories or just being interested in us, but love is love.' – Heath Ledger

Ledger's 'earthy charisma' wasn't enough to make *Ned Kelly* a success at the box office. The movie grossed a mere $75,000, with takings of £211,000 in the UK. (It did score over $6 million outside the US, mainly in Australia, where it was a big hit.) The *Hollywood Reporter*'s fears proved accurate: US audiences were simply not interested in an Australian folk hero, even if he was played by pin-up Heath Ledger.

By August 2002, Heath's relationship with his *Ned Kelly* co-star, Naomi Watts, was big news. Both had returned to Hollywood after wrapping the movie, and the pair had been seen out and about, enjoying intimate dinners and late morning breakfasts at various LA eateries.

Orlando Bloom had reputedly played matchmaker for the pair in Australia, and then colluded with Ledger to keep the relationship under wraps when they returned to the States. The young Australian appeared to have learned from his very public relationship with Heather Graham. Bloom would be seen out on the town with Ledger, only for Ledger to hook up with a waiting Watts once the pair had entered the VIP room of that night's LA club. One member of their inner circle was quoted as

'It turned out to be one of the easiest roles I've had to play,
because I found something in him to hold onto – a few thoughts that
carried me through the whole movie. And once you find something like
that, something you can really trust, you can do anything.'
– Heath Ledger

Left: *Ned and Julia (Naomi Watts) embark upon a dangerous liaison.*
Above: *'Shooting many of the scenes was fairly eerie because we were
capturing a piece of time,' Heath said of* Ned Kelly.

saying, 'Orlando loved being part of it. He'd arrive at nightclubs with Heath knowing that once inside the VIP room, he'd be dumped for Naomi. He thought it was a hoot.'

But, tellingly, Ledger's attempt to reconnect with Sean Combs (his fellow supporting cast member in *Monster's Ball*), at the Vogue/VH1 Fashion Awards at New York's Lotus club in October 2002, saw a fracas when the rap star's bouncers failed to recognise the actor and refused him access. It was only when they recognised Naomi Watts that everything was resolved.

'I know it's weird that I'm such a private person but still date high-profile women,' Heath candidly stated of the relationship. 'But I can't let the celebrity thing influence my decisions on who I see; that would be unfair to myself.'

By November 2002, the UK's *Daily Mirror* was reporting that, not only had the pair moved into Ledger's new Hollywood home together, they were planning to get married – possibly even before Christmas. It would have been a big step, but, going by Heath's response to the rumour, it seemed an unlikely prospect.

'Naomi may be living with me, but I've lived in my house for eight months since I bought it four years ago. So that gives you an idea of what my life's like.' – Heath Ledger

'I've already lived all over the place and it's likely that I'll carry on moving around. And that's no way to conduct anything as serious as marriage,' he insisted. 'Naomi may be living with me, but I've lived in my house for eight months since I bought it four years ago . . . We're just trying to catch up with each other all the time. As for the eleven-year age gap, it makes no difference. I'm interested in the person, not the age of that person.'

The Ledger-Watts romance turned out to be somewhat tempestuous. By February 2003, it appeared that the couple had split. Although the separation was only temporary, maybe, despite his protestations to the contrary, the prospect of marrying an actress eleven years his senior was causing him to get cold feet. (After all, as events would illustrate, his penchant for older women would soon be a thing of the past.) 'I still have so much to do,' he justified his hesitation. 'It'd be unfair to commit to marriage. And my parents divorced when I was ten, so I can't say I have the greatest faith in marriage.'

March 2003 saw Heath and Naomi put the public interest in their erratic union to positive use when they appeared side-by-side at an anti-war rally in Melbourne, during which tens of thousands of people peacefully marched against the American invasion of Iraq.

When quizzed about the damage such a stance might inflict upon his career, Heath bluntly replied, 'At the end of the day my career is so insignificant in this war, it just is, and I'm willing to lose a few jobs over it.' He went on to say of the war: 'It is not a fight for humanity. It is a fight for oil and screw it and screw them. I think we should all pull out and leave a peaceful existence down here.'

By June of that year, the couple were back together again in Vancouver, where Watts was filming *We Don't Live Here Anymore* with Laura Dern. The following month Ledger was due back in Prague, to start filming on Terry Gilliam's *The*

Brothers Grimm. In September, Ledger and Watts were reportedly house-hunting in New York and Los Angeles. Naomi addressed the problem of them both filming separately at different times: 'Being apart so much is horrible. But then we are not normal people and we don't crave the regularity of nine to five that comes with that.'

They may not have had (or wanted) 'regularity', but issues like marriage and children eventually conspired to drive them apart. Naomi was keen on having children, but 24-year-old Heath was simply not ready to settle down. Ms Watts confessed her desire: 'I'm dying to have a child and we'd like to have kids at some point. But right now we're both busy with our careers.'

The regular separation caused by their work led to another split being publicly confirmed in September, only for the pair to reunite once again in December in order to attend Heath's sister Kate's wedding to her long-term partner at a secret location in Perth.

Despite this sequence of temporary separations, the two actors were still going out with each other in March 2004, having reconnected between films, desperate to make the relationship work. However, the subject of children was still at the forefront of Naomi's mind, according to an interview in *W* magazine. '[My mother] is dying for me to have children and, quite frankly, I've been dying for it since I was nineteen, but I hadn't met the right man . . . At the age of 35, my career couldn't be going better, but we all know that fertility slows down at this point, so it's about making choices. I really do want to experience a baby.'

Having attempted to keep the press at bay, Ledger hit out when he felt the detailed coverage of the on-again/off-again romance was too intrusive. 'People try to make it challenging for us by assuming and creating stories or just being interested in us, but love is love. If you're in love, it's easy and it's hard in a good way. Our relationship is everything a healthy relationship should be.'

He also claimed he hated being the centre of attention, especially when it didn't relate to his work. 'It's the worst part of the job. It's a surreal experience to be hounded or followed or recognised. But at least I'm not Michael Jackson.'

Finally, in May 2004, the Ledger-Watts show finally came to an end. Earlier in the month, she had complained to Heath about his open flirtation with actress Scarlett Johansson in an LA nightclub. By mid-month, the final split was official. Ms Watts' publicist confirmed the pair had gone their separate ways, but refused to comment on the reasons behind their break-up. However, sources close to the couple blamed 35-year-old Naomi's waning affections on the now 25-year-old Ledger's wild lifestyle and wandering eye. While Ms Watts was keen to settle down and start a family, she had come to believe that Heath was not yet ready for such responsibility. And Ledger had, by then, not only been publicly connected with Scarlett Johansson, but with Winona Ryder too.

At almost two years, however, his relationship with Naomi Watts had been his longest to date. It had survived their work schedules and age difference, but her desire to settle down and have children had finally doomed it. Naomi described their break-up as sad, but inevitable: 'I think deep down we both knew there wasn't a forever plan.' She concluded, however, that she had absolutely no regrets about

the time they'd spent together. 'I have nothing but good things to say about Heath Ledger. We loved each other. I'm close with his family; he's close with mine. He is a friend and we'll always remain in contact.'

'I never sit around and think about my career that much,' Heath claimed. 'I'm a pretty lazy person. I don't really sit around and get all calculated about everything.' His laidback approach to his seemingly failing career went hand-in-hand with his disdainful attitude to film stardom. 'I tend to not believe my position in the whole system,' he said of the star-making process. 'I don't believe myself to be an invincible power. I don't believe myself to be of supernatural quality. I know I'm just a regular person and I hold onto that.'

His critical analysis of the most recent films he had made (with the notable exception of *Ned Kelly*) was hard-hitting. 'I still haven't secured a position as an actor who can act,' he claimed, conscious of his status as a mere 'movie star' figure. 'I've done some crappy shit, and I haven't showcased myself yet.'

'You've got to be careful; you've got to map out your career and stay true to that. Had I listened to my agent, I'd be running around in tights, climbing buildings and stuff.'
– Heath Ledger

In fact, he wasn't even sure if he wanted to continue acting as a career, so difficult was it to find good work within the Hollywood system. 'I don't know what my goals are. I don't know if I want to do it for the rest of my life. I've never been someone to do one thing. I don't know if I could do just one thing.'

And he had a definite alternative career plan in mind. Photography had been a serious hobby for a long time, something he found himself becoming ever more obsessed with. 'I guess it's the capturing of "essence",' he said of his photographic work. 'It's capturing the piece of light bouncing off of a moment. It's more documenting my life, what I feel and see. It started off as putting together a visual diary, but I also do photo art. I blow up prints, paint on them and scratch on them.'

Ledger knew there was more to life than becoming a movie star, but he had learned an important lesson. 'You've got to realise the power of saying "No",' he said. 'It's what you say "Yes" to that ultimately shapes you. One way I manage is to not take the film industry completely seriously while at the same time taking my craft seriously. There is a life outside acting, I won't let it overtake my life.'

It was an idea that Heath Ledger was increasingly warming to: if his career was sabotaged by a lack of credible roles, perhaps he should just quit altogether? After all, life had so much more to offer a relatively wealthy 25-year-old.

'I get a lot of joy and pleasure out of life, full stop. I work to live, and that's the only reason why I work, so I wouldn't think twice about stopping.'

Naomi Watts and Heath attend the 76th Annual Academy Awards in 2004.
After meeting on the set of Ned Kelly, *the couple stayed together for two years.*

4. FORCE OF NATURE

'I needed to go out and make some bad movies and some
interesting movies that weren't based on safe box-office choices.
I needed to cleanse myself of this commercial filth that was
being injected into me. I needed to be reborn.'
– Heath Ledger

'My success, early on, was manufactured,' claimed Heath as he prepared to take charge of his own destiny. 'The studios found this kid, they put him in a movie. They're like, "Let's put his face on a poster. Let's put him on the cover of these magazines. Let's turn him into a star." I wasn't ready for it. I felt like I hadn't done anything to deserve it. I couldn't act!'

Ledger's method of escaping the studio straitjacket was a form of self-destruction and reconstruction. 'I needed to go out and make some bad movies and some interesting movies that weren't based on safe box-office choices,' he conceded. 'I almost didn't want them to make money . . . I wanted to destroy it all and shake it all up, and go, "Back off, leave me alone. I'm gonna do this, I'm gonna do that, and you're gonna hate all of it." I needed to cleanse myself of this commercial filth that was being injected into me. I needed to be reborn.'

But he wasn't rushing into it without a plan. He was prepared to learn from experience and by analysing his past mistakes. 'When I started to watch some of the films I'd done, I realised I was doing movies that I might not actually want to see,' Ledger admitted candidly. 'I thought, I need to be more cautious about my choices – it reflects on who I am. So I became more respectful of that. It dawned on me that my choices would dictate my future.'

Throughout 2004 and into the early part of 2005, he would tackle a diverse set of films, from the knockabout fantasy of *The Brothers Grimm* to the stoner biography *Lords of Dogtown* (in which he played a real-life character), via the challenging, highly acclaimed *Brokeback Mountain*, back to the fun and frolics of *Casanova*, and finally the downbeat drug romance *Candy*. Ledger chose a series of roles to showcase his versatility, allowing him to bring to life a much wider range

Heath's dissatisfaction with the movie industry was fuelled by self-doubt.
'I still haven't secured a position as an actor who can act,' he claimed.

of characters than he had become known for.

'It's definitely given me hope,' he said of his work during this period. 'I think before that I was really bored with the choices I made and with the movies. It was starting to get stale and I was on a plateau. This was my year to handpick things for the first time. I really wanted to put together a collection of quality work.'

It would also be a period when a new romance coincided with his growing stardom, and the kind of uncontrolled press attention that this inevitably brings.

When director Terry Gilliam had to cast the leads for his movie based on the lives and work of the legendary Grimm brothers, he had just two actors in mind. Will Grimm had to be a smart, hard-nosed con artist out to make a living, while his brother Jacob is a wide-eyed dreamer who still believes in the magic of fairy tales.

'Matt [Damon] and Heath were obviously the heart of the movie for me,' explained Gilliam, 'but at first I thought Matt would play Jake, because he's usually more of an introspective and sensitive character and Heath would play Will, because he's usually cast as the straight-ahead hero. Matt came into our first meeting and said he wanted to play Will. I wasn't sure about it at first, but then Heath came to me and said, "Well, I'd like to play Jake." Then I realised this was absolutely the right thing, because I love to cast against type.'

'This was my year to handpick things for the first time. I really wanted to put together a collection of quality work.' – Heath Ledger

Gilliam had been developing his fairytale movie for several years. 'Fairy tales are my kind of world,' he said. 'We had a script I really believed in. The idea was to create very real characters in a real world, then these strange and scary fairytale elements begin to intrude and take over.'

The Brothers Grimm would depict Will and Jacob, the writers behind the classic fairy tales, as travellers in the Napoleonic countryside, faking the presence of monsters and demons that they'd quickly vanquish (in exchange for some easy money, of course).

But what would happen if the brothers found themselves involved in a real-life fairy tale, complete with demonic queens and monsters? Gilliam's film weaves elements of 'Cinderella', 'Little Red Riding Hood', 'Hansel and Gretel' and other tales into the story, as the brothers confront a fantastic reality beyond their imagination.

'We've created a fairy tale about the brothers Grimm, in which they at first appear to be hip and heroic, but we quickly learn it is all a con,' said Gilliam. 'Soon they're caught up in a world that is exactly like the tales the Grimms have been collecting: their reality becomes entwined with fantasy.'

Attracting Heath Ledger to take part in Gilliam's fantasy epic wasn't easy, as the actor had been determined to take a break from acting. 'I'd quite literally told my agent not to call me. Don't send me anything. I don't want to know about it,' said Ledger. 'I wanted to have some personal time.'

However, the approach from Terry Gilliam resulted in a change of mind. 'At

'Filming in Prague felt like we were actually in a fairy tale because it is so gothic and medieval. The buildings were all bent out of shape and so it felt like we were in a Gilliam world anyway.' – Heath Ledger

Grimm and Grimmer. Jacob (Heath) and Will (Matt Damon) prepare to do battle with the forces of evil in Terry Gilliam's fantasy adventure The Brothers Grimm *(2005).*

Heath and actress Lena Headey in a scene from The Brothers Grimm. *The film's shoot took place in Prague and lasted for 110 days.*

'Terry Gilliam was the first director who saw me for what I could do. He challenged me and I was ready to earn my career and start over, essentially.' – Heath Ledger

that point I'd been in a really self-destructive mode with my career – quite intentionally, actually,' Ledger told *Entertainment Weekly*. 'I wasn't doing anything that was testing me. Terry was the first director who saw me for what I could do. He challenged me and I was ready to earn my career and start over, essentially.'

'When we began moving forward on *Grimm*, [cinematographer] Nicola Pecorini was shooting a film in Rome with Heath playing the lead, *The Order*,' recalled Gilliam of his initial interest in Ledger. 'So Nicola called me and said, "This kid I'm working with, he's great! He's really good!" He reminded Nicola of Johnny Depp, the same kind of quality: he was dangerous, fearless. I met Heath in LA, and he was very different than the kind of characters he's played. He couldn't stop moving and was nervous and twitching.'

Ledger said of his director, 'I always thought he has a brilliant mind. I sat down with Terry when I first met him, and my hands just go everywhere, when I'm nervous or if I'm talking. They go faster than my mind. I was that way in front of Terry. He started giggling. I thought, "What's he giggling about?" He's like, "That's great, what you're doing is great. That's what I want."'

The swapping of roles was the key to Ledger's involvement, said Gilliam. 'Matt's always been more introspective, the more intelligent, the quieter, the more intense actor and Heath has played these bigger parts where he's the leading man.

It's great that we did the swap because they're far, far more interesting. Heath is someone the world is used to seeing as a more conventional hero, but here you see that he also has another kind of nervous side to him that's very intriguing.'

Ledger's Jake Grimm is the sentimental believer in fairy tales, who thinks the enchanted worlds he has always secretly believed in might really exist. 'This role was a real opportunity to leap out of my skin,' he said of his decision to come out of a self-imposed hiatus in the late summer of 2003. 'It's a comic role and Terry gave me the gift of allowing me to feel comfortable and free enough to go to extremes and really express myself. He gave us the opportunity to create these characters that we hadn't been given the opportunity to do in the past. I had the time of my life doing it.'

'I think Terry Gilliam is brilliant and he's such a nice guy. I'm not interested in working with genius bastards. And with Terry, I don't really care what the project is. I'd work on anything he wanted me for.' – Heath Ledger

Heath quickly hit it off with Matt Damon. 'It's a real personal process,' he said, 'how you become someone's brother in a flash. We tried out a lot of different ways to synchronise with each other, how to smile like each other, laugh like each other. We observed each other's characteristics and movements to make those similar. The idea was always to have some similarities and a lot of really huge contrasts – as brothers often do.'

Heath and Matt spent a lot of time talking and drinking beer together. 'That's the sort of stuff that really creates an authentic feeling of brotherhood,' Matt acknowledged. 'Befriending each other wasn't hard. We had four weeks before shooting the film where we were doing accents and horse riding. It was just shaping our characters. We were in Prague, so we'd all go out to dinner and hang out. We'd actually go bowl every Friday and Saturday night with pretty much most of the crew.'

Gilliam had searched the countryside around the Prague studio to find the ideal village for his movie, but failed. The solution was an entire fantasy village built from scratch. In addition to the village of Marbaden, production designer Guy Dyas also created locations such as a torture chamber and the Rapunzel-like Tower of Charot (which houses Monica Bellucci's deceptive witch-queen). The Barrandov studio back lot was pressed into service to house a variety of fantastical locations, bringing to life the fairytale worlds of *The Brothers Grimm*.

While Ledger found the convincing sets helped him get into the character of Jake Grimm, he found even greater inspiration from his director. 'I allowed myself to go a little cuckoo once we started shooting. A lot of it came from Terry's energy. I started to mimic him a little bit. Terry gives you the opportunity to step outside of yourself. He dares you to be bad.'

Unlike Gilliam's previous, uncompleted project, *The Man Who Killed Don Quixote*, *The Brothers Grimm* was a relatively hassle-free, straightforward shoot, taking around 110 days before wrapping in November 2003. For his part, Ledger was glad the maverick director had helped him get over his recent career crisis. 'I am a dreamer,' he accepted. 'I've always been easily cast as the "hero" but that's always been very boring to me. That's why it was a brilliant opportunity to play at this pace. For the first time, I wasn't being asked to suck in my energy. I did not have to tie my hands down. I could express [myself]. So I did. On top of that, I ate a shit-load of chocolate throughout the shoot to keep me hyperactive. That was the key [to my performance], chocolate!'

Upon its release in August 2005, *The Brothers Grimm* met with the accusation of prioritising style over substance that many of Gilliam's movies had encountered. Manohla Dargis, in the *New York Times*, suggested the director badly served his two stars, Damon and Ledger, who were required to 'shout their lines and run circles around each other as they try to advance the plot'. However, some critics did take a liking to the movie. Ty Burr, in the *Boston Globe*, called it 'an absurd mess that's more entertaining than it has any right to be'. And at least one critic simply loved the movie: Jim Fusilli, in the *Wall Street Journal*, called *The Brothers Grimm* 'a wildly wondrous reinvention of the story of the chroniclers of dark, occasionally horrific, child-pleasing fairy tales . . . a celebration of the power of stories'.

The movie had sat unreleased for about a year after completion, caught up in the battle between Miramax co-owners Bob and Harvey Weinstein and the company's new studio partner, Disney. (It would finally see the light of day immediately prior to the brothers' final departure from the company they founded.) It debuted at Number 2 on the box-office chart, and took just over $15 million on its opening weekend, but went on to gross just under $38 million in the US (a disappointing return against an estimated budget of $80 million).

'Heath is someone who the world is used to seeing as a more conventional hero, but here you see that he also has another kind of nervous, quiet side to him that's very intriguing.' – Terry Gilliam

Making *The Brothers Grimm* had given Heath a whole new perspective on his acting career. He now had a game-plan. 'I did four or five films over the last eighteen months including this [*Grimm*],' he said. 'I guess I was heading down a path where it was starting to get difficult to find good material and good people to work with. So I thought, "Screw this." I just wanted to show what I could do, many different colours of myself. I picked four different stories and four really diverse characters to portray. From *Grimm* to *Lords of Dogtown* and *Brokeback Mountain*, then *Casanova*.' It was a proactive decision that would eventually lead to his career-defining performance in *Brokeback Mountain*.

Heath had film executive Amy Pascal to thank for his role in *Lords of Dogtown*. When she was at Columbia, she'd parachuted him straight into the lead in *A Knight's Tale* after seeing his work on *The Patriot*. They had battled over Ledger's role in the promotion of the jousting movie, but still remained friends. Now chairman of Sony Pictures, Ms Pascal was a confirmed admirer of Heath's talents.

Lords of Dogtown was a screenplay about skateboarding, based on a 1999 article from *Spin* magazine and an acclaimed 2002 documentary called *Dogtown and*

Perma-stoned skateboarding guru Skip Engblom (Heath) takes a barefoot ride through 1970s Santa Monica in true-life drama Lords of Dogtown *(2005).*

Z-Boys. It dramatised the lives of a gang of poor kids from Santa Monica who made a fortune through their board skills, a classic American success story with an edge.

Stacy Peralta, a member of the original gang featured in *Dogtown and Z-Boys*, had written and directed the documentary. 'We used to ride walls as if we were surfing them,' recalled Peralta. 'That's how the whole Z-Boy thing developed. We were surfers first who took all our drive and ambition and motivation to become professional surfers and switched it to become professional skateboarders.'

Peralta also scripted the Hollywood movie version. Everyone involved – including director Catherine Hardwicke – agreed that authenticity would be the key to its success, and so decided to hire as many of the original gang as possible as both skaters and technical consultants. World-renowned skating champion Tony Alva took on the task of choreographing stunts and teaching the actors to skate in true Z-Boy fashion.

Hiring appropriate actors was next on the agenda. Amy Pascal suggested Ledger for the part of Skip Engblom, co-owner of the Zephyr Shop, where the gang bought their skating supplies. 'Skip was the scout leader. He was there to cheer you up or kick you in the ass, depending on what you needed at the time,' said Z-Boy Wentzle Ruml IV of the real-life Engblom.

It was through Skip that the Z-Boys gang found fame, and, from the moment he heard about the movie, Engblom agreed with Pascal that only one guy could play him. 'I saw this kid in *The Patriot*,' explained Engblom, 'and when people started asking me who I thought should play me, I said it should be Heath Ledger. Everyone always said it would never happen because he was too big. When Catherine [Hardwicke] became attached as director, they asked me again, and again I said, "Heath Ledger." Catherine called me a few weeks later and said, "Guess who's gonna play you in the movie?" and I said, "Whoopi Goldberg?" She said, "No, Heath Ledger." I couldn't believe it.'

'I just wanted to show what I could do, many different colours of myself. I picked four different stories and four really diverse characters to portray. From *Grimm* to *Lords of Dogtown* and *Brokeback Mountain*, then *Casanova*.' – Heath Ledger

Ledger had seen the original documentary, and was attracted by the surfer attitude of the skaters. It was something he could relate to directly. 'I left my hometown of Perth when I was sixteen and I stopped surfing then with the exception of two or three times a year,' he said. 'This movie seemed like a wonderful excuse to get back out there.'

Although disappointed that his career had not been revitalised by *Ned Kelly*, and worried about the effect that taking a supporting role might have, Heath was persuaded by Amy Pascal to meet Engblom. 'Heath and I met and it was very strange how similar we are,' said Engblom. 'I liked him right away. We'd go to Laker games and hang out a lot. Heath wanted to get to know me and my mannerisms.'

Playing a living character was a new challenge for Heath. 'I realised it was going to be an honour to play Skip, particularly after meeting him,' he said. 'He's such a rich character and a beautiful human being to portray, and that was really the clincher for me taking the role.'

When trying on Engblom's actual skating gear from the 1970s, Heath found that the outfits fitted him perfectly. Once filming began, his subject kept away from him, to allow the actor to absorb and employ what he'd learned from their time together. 'Heath is a brilliant actor,' praised Engblom. 'He didn't need me to tell him how to be me. It would be like standing over a great artist and telling him to add more blue in the corner of the painting. I didn't watch one scene [being filmed] the entire time.'

Lords of Dogtown was shot entirely on location in Southern California in 56 days, at locations ranging from quirky Imperial Beach (standing in for the now renovated Venice Beach), San Pedro (where the Zephyr Shop was recreated) and a custom-built 'dogbowl' to stand in for the kidney-shaped swimming pool where the gang skated in Pacific Palisades. The recreation of 1970s locations certainly convinced original Z-Boy and screenwriter Peralta. 'All of the kids looked like we did in the 1970s . . . It was a very *Twilight Zone* experience!'

'If I was to go out and play safe and do movies which I know are going to make money every time, then I'm just going to make boring fucking movies.' – Heath Ledger

Released in September 2005, *Lords of Dogtown* had a decent $5.6 million opening weekend but could only climb to a disappointing cumulative total of $11 million, against a production budget of around $25 million. The *Chicago Sun-Times'* Roger Ebert felt there was no need for the movie to exist, considering that the previous documentary had adequately covered the material: 'Nobody in the fiction film pulls off stunts as spectacular as those we see for real in the documentary. Heath Ledger plays Skip, the mentor who sponsors the Zephyr Team, gives them their first priceless T-shirts and eventually, stoned and drunk, ends up making surfboards in somebody else's back room. He was the catalyst. There were a lot of drugs around; although we see Skip here as a survivor, he's more of a victim.'

Variety was equally dismissive. 'It's a wipe-out once the pic skids into melodrama and an overly schematic sense of how success tore the group apart,' wrote Robert Koehler. '*Lords* remains superficial and disconcertingly conventional. Nearly unrecognisable at first, Ledger's Skip goes from gruff stoner boss to a pathetic shell of a man, but the change isn't always convincing.' *Rolling Stone's* Peter Travers thought *Lords of Dogtown* 'a frenzy of crazy-cool board action' that failed because 'slippery-slope-of-success clichés halt the film's momentum. [But] Heath Ledger is flamboyantly funny and alive as Z-Boys guru Skip Engblom.'

Ledger's response to criticism of *Lords of Dogtown* had a familiar tone. 'It's not like it really kind of stabbed me in any way,' he said of the movie. 'It's like if I was to go out and play safe and do movies which I know are going to make money every time, then I'm just going to make boring fucking movies. I'd rather take the risk of making a movie that's not going to be commercially successful and may not be good but may be brilliant, I'd rather take those risks.'

His next film would see Ledger take the biggest risk of his career – and result in his greatest triumph.

Ang Lee directs Heath and co-star Jake Gyllenhaal before filming a key scene from the elegiac, Oscar-winning Brokeback Mountain (2005).

'It transcends a label. It's a story of two human beings who are in love; get over the fact that it's two men – that's the point.' – Heath Ledger

Brokeback Mountain was a very lonely experience and it was supposed to be,' said Heath of his critically acclaimed performance as Ennis Del Mar, in director Ang Lee's 'gay Western'.

'My character was extremely lonely and I think I carried that through the whole experience. [Ang Lee and Terry Gilliam] are both wonderful directors and they definitely both have the same level of attention to detail. Sometimes Ang will be like, "Okay, drag cigarette. Okay, blow out. Okay, look at mountain. Okay, now look at feet. Look back at mountain. Okay." You try to take this in, make it look natural. Terry does that too in a way. He'll yell out things to you, but it's kind of in different tones. Terry laughs a lot more.'

The transition from the wild, imaginative environment of *The Brothers Grimm* to portraying a real-life skater-slacker in *Lords of Dogtown* and the introspective, quietly internal acting required for *Brokeback Mountain* was quite a change of pace – and it was exactly the kind of dramatic challenge he was searching for.

The film was based on a short story by Pulitzer Prize-winning author Annie Proulx, adapted for the screen by the team of fellow Pulitzer winner Larry McMurtry and his writing partner Diana Ossana. Set against the sweeping landscapes and bleak plains of Wyoming and Texas, the film tells the story of two young men – a ranch-hand and a rodeo cowboy – who meet in the summer of 1963 and unexpectedly form a powerful emotional attachment that endures throughout the rest of their lives.

'To me, *Brokeback Mountain* is uniquely, and universally, a great American love story,' said director Ang Lee, who may have seemed like an odd choice for this intimate tale, given that his most recent movie had been comic-book action-adventure flop *Hulk*. However, Lee had previously helmed such diverse films as *Sense and Sensibility*, the 1970s relationship drama *The Ice Storm* and American Civil War movie *Ride with the Devil*.

Screenwriters McMurtry and Ossana, sensing the cinematic potential, had optioned the screen rights to the slight short story with their own money. 'We wrote the screenplay in less than three months,' said Ossana, '[then] tried for nearly seven years to get it into production. Various directors came on board at different times, and several actors wanted to be in the film, but no actors would commit.'

'It was a beautiful story. It was a story that hadn't made it onto the screen; it is rare to come upon a script so beautifully well written that hadn't been told before. I never saw it as the huge risk that everyone else was seeing.' – Heath Ledger

The prejudice against gay roles in American movies was still evident when it came to casting. Despite Tom Hanks and Antonio Banderas starring in 1993's *Philadelphia*, gay characters were still associated with minor character actors, and often with the subject of AIDS. It didn't help when, early in his career, Will Smith refused to kiss another man on screen in *Six Degrees of Separation*. (It was a stance the actor would later regret.) As a result of this general atmosphere, casting two young actors in the central roles of *Brokeback Mountain* proved to be a major challenge.

'As powerful as the story and script were,' noted Ossana, 'with good parts for actors, I knew that it would take actors who were smart and brave to commit to this and go places emotionally that they'd never gone before, and who would be willing to make this challenging movie on a modest budget.'

With Lee on board as director, the project received a fresh impetus. 'I decided to take a risk and go with a younger cast,' said Lee of his approach to the material. 'It's a twenty-year story, and you cannot recreate youth easily. I decided to go with [actors in their] younger twenties. The young have innocence and freshness, and believe in what they're doing. They make the effort, and you don't over-instruct them. Nothing's more rewarding for a filmmaker than when young actors listen and [then] come [up] with great results.'

But which young actors would take on the roles? Who would be willing to put their reputation on the line, yet would still be enough of a draw to make the movie a success with a mainstream audience? First to sign on was Jake Gyllenhaal. 'I was immediately drawn to *Brokeback Mountain* because love stories haven't been told this way,' Gyllenhaal recalled. 'Movies avoided the struggles and the trials that it takes to actually be in love. When I heard that Ang Lee was going to make it, I thought, "I have to do this movie."'

The main characters are ranch-hand Ennis Del Mar and rodeo cowboy Jack Twist, who meet on Brokeback Mountain and unexpectedly fall in love. The film charts the pair's struggle to deal with their feelings, their families and the social attitudes of the time, while furtively indulging their forbidden passion on infrequent 'fishing trips'. The production had found their Jack, but filling the cowboy boots of Ennis was a whole other problem. The role, as written, had very specific requirements. '"Ennis" means "island,"' explained co-star Anne Hathaway. 'Ennis is a man unto himself, and he keeps to himself the most of anybody in *Brokeback Mountain* – and affects people. He can't access his emotions and be with the person he loves most in the entire world.'

'If you just be safe about the choices you make, you don't grow.' – Heath Ledger

Heath Ledger, looking for roles that would force him to raise his game dramatically, was automatically attracted to *Brokeback Mountain*. 'It was a beautiful story. It was a story that hadn't made it on the screen; it is rare to come upon a script so beautifully well written and that hadn't been told before. It was very exciting to tell a new story . . . I looked at it as a wonderful opportunity to get in the head of this character. I never saw it as the huge risk that everyone else was seeing. It's all relative to the person you are and how relaxed you are with the people around you.'

So keen was Ledger to secure the role, he agreed to take on the character of Ennis Del Mar without either talking or meeting with Ang Lee. 'I trusted that story in Ang's hands,' he said of his impetuous response. 'There were so many actors in the past seven years who have been attached to *Brokeback Mountain*, yet who have been convinced by their managers, agents, publicists, or all three combined, not to do it, because it would ruin their career. I was approached to make the movie, maybe because I was the last on the list, but I didn't think twice about it.'

Screenwriter McMurtry was instantly sold on the idea of the actor playing Ennis. 'Diana [Ossana] asked that I watch the first twenty minutes of *Monster's Ball* to see Heath's performance. That's the only performance of his I'd seen. After seeing him in that role, I felt certain that he had what it would take to play Ennis Del Mar – he was that powerful.'

For Lee's part, he was happy to have finally found his second leading man. 'I feel very fortunate to have Heath in the movie,' said Lee. 'He's a natural. He has great co-ordination, he's very dedicated, and he does his preparation. He meticulously aims towards a certain target and firmly believes in what he's doing.'

Perhaps a bigger negative factor (at least for ego-driven actors) than the gay angle was the lack of dialogue for Ennis. 'Heath and I talked about how Ennis doesn't speak much,' explained Lee. 'Deep inside, he has a big fear from a childhood traumatic experience, and from his awakening to his own sexuality. Ennis has to cover that up with his attitude and, sometimes, violence. He can get very violent, because of how scared he is. So he's a scared kid inside, playing a Western kind of cool. Heath not only had to carry his own character and the whole character of the West, but carry the movie – and he underplayed powerfully.'

Reflecting his new embrace of challenging roles, Ledger saw his character's laconic nature as simply another chance to develop his craft and stretch his ability. 'I actually thought it was a gift not to have words to play with,' he said. 'I wanted to make it physical, as that was all I was really left with . . . I think any form of expression had to be painful. I wanted him to be a clenched fist; therefore my mouth became clenched too. A lot of this was lack of posture, but with the lack of posture in his mouth; in the words, it escapes his mouth.'

This was clearly the most demanding, complex role of Ledger's career so far. Ennis was an internalised character and, in figuring out how to bring him to life on screen, Heath found himself absorbing much of Ennis's rage and conflict within himself. As this new stage of his career progressed, he would sometimes find it hard to drop aspects of his character after filming. And so he would use the gaps between films to re-orient himself to 'real' life, as opposed to 'reel' life, before starting all over again. Ultimately, however, Heath's obsessive immersion in his own method would cause great problems both for himself and those closest to him.

'You're affected by whatever you're portraying,' he acknowledged. 'Your body has a memory of the experiences you have in life. If you're tricking yourself to feel anger every day, you go home angry. Then you get home, and you're like, "Argh! Fuck me, why am I angry? I've got no reason to be angry." And you wind yourself down again. But you do carry it. The mood of a film always takes me over.'

'He's easy to photograph, easier than Jake. With some actors, you have to avoid this and that. Not with Heath.' – Ang Lee

Trapped in the wilderness of Calgary, Canada, shooting *Brokeback Mountain*, there had been no escape from the loneliness and isolation that Ennis felt. 'The second I would lie down to go to sleep and close my eyes, I'm going through what happened the whole day all over again. Every take, every single thing: I recollect everything. You don't stop thinking about it, don't stop carrying it around, and that is pretty hard. I feel like a sponge when I'm working.'

But taking a character across a twenty-year time period was a prospect that he relished. 'Physically ageing between eighteen and 40 is fairly slim and subtle, but for Ennis, he didn't really evolve emotionally either,' Heath observed. 'I used my accent to adapt the tone of voice at the beginning when he's younger; it's pitched a little higher and it's a little more energetic and enthusiastic. It slowly gets deeper and raspier, more fixed and tighter towards the end. I thought that was just a subtle vehicle I could use to age.'

As in almost every movie he made, Heath's horse-riding experience was put to good use. 'The easiest thing I found was being a ranch-hand, being a horse back-up. I can ride backwards if I had to. I'm very comfortable with horses and grew up around farm-hands. Even though I was born in Perth, Western Australia, there's something very universal about anyone who's on horseback night and day. There's a universal trait. Even physically, when you are on horseback night and day, when you

'My biggest anxiety wasn't having to kiss Jake. It was a perfect script and Ang Lee was the perfect director. So the anxiety for me was – I didn't want to be the one to fuck it up. And I was willing to do anything.'
– Heath Ledger

'Obviously *Brokeback Mountain* was an obstacle
I felt I could never climb, I could never defeat, that it was too tough but ultimately decided to do it. And with that I came out with a real sense of accomplishment, which was something that I lacked in the movies that I've done before; I'd never felt that
I'd accomplished anything.'
– Heath Ledger

Left and above: *Ennis (Heath) fights a losing battle against his feelings for Jack (Jake Gyllenhaal) during their twenty-year affair in the iconic* Brokeback Mountain, *for which Heath was awarded a Best Actor Oscar nomination.*

get off that horse, you are still walking as if there's still a horse between your legs.'

Jake Gyllenhaal found himself intimidated by Ledger's horse craft. 'Heath has known how to ride since he was a kid, and he's already done movies where he's ridden a horse. I knew nothing about riding horses. I came up a month before we started shooting, for, as we called it, "cowboy training camp". I learned how to ride horses, how to wrangle sheep, and how to do the cowboy things.'

According to Lee, Gyllenhaal's co-star wasn't above a little refresher course: 'Heath went [to camp], too. He and Jake needed to feel comfortable and find a chemistry – and Jake needed to get blisters and bloody hands, chopping wood, hauling bales of hay, putting up fences . . .'

One thing Ledger managed to avoid was a series of preparation sessions in the gym. 'Ang really wanted me to build up,' the actor admitted. 'He wanted me to get bigger and stronger. I was trying to convince him that masculinity comes from maturity. I thought that Ennis was a poor dirt ranch-hand. He doesn't go to the gym and he certainly doesn't eat big meals. In fact, when you get older, you get thinner. I thought he would look more desolate and lonely than someone [who] would be in a Calvin Klein commercial.'

As well as being enthused and engaged afresh by the challenge of *Brokeback Mountain*, the final piece of main casting was to change Ledger's life dramatically.

Michelle Williams signed on to play the expanded role of Alma, the wife of Ennis. Heath had only recently made the final break from Naomi Watts, one month prior to the film's June–August 2004 shoot. Now, just as he had during the making of *Ned Kelly*, he would fall for his leading lady – although, at age 24, Ms Williams was younger than his previous girlfriends.

'There are not actually love scenes for the sake of doing a love scene. There are actually stories within each of those moments.' – Heath Ledger

Heath claimed that his feelings surfaced during the first scene he and Michelle shot together, when she fell off a toboggan and injured her knee. 'Michelle was coming through a difficult phase,' he said of the woman who was to change his life. 'She had no idea how beautiful she is, how talented. Her gaze was downcast, like Ennis's. She'd been acting professionally since she was eight, and going to auditions. Never being sure why you're rejected or accepted makes you insecure and vulnerable.'

Given how significant a moment it was to be in his life, it's no surprise that Heath had a strong visual memory of the incident. 'We were knee-deep in snow,' he recalled of the shoot. 'On the fifth take, Michelle and I were tobogganing down the hill, and we were supposed to fall off. We were having a fun time, then Michelle was screaming in pain. I thought, "She's acting," but she really was in pain. She'd twisted her knee and she was pretty much on crutches for the rest of the shoot. I felt I always had to look after her after that.'

Ledger accompanied Williams in the ambulance that took her to hospital following the accident. However, he didn't regard himself as coming to her rescue: it was a mutual process. 'She rescued me as much as I rescued her,' Heath joked.

'Michelle has strengths where I have weaknesses, and she gave me a real life. I love how her posture has changed, her gaze now is up.'

Director Ang Lee could quickly see the direction the relationship was heading in. 'Heath was all worked up, holding her hands, and wanted to go to hospital,' Lee said. He watched the relationship grow quickly during the shoot. 'It started happening shortly after rehearsal. I know Heath had just broken up with Naomi [Watts]. And of course, I kept pushing him towards Jake.'

For his part, co-star Jake Gyllenhaal saw the writing on the wall, too. 'I remember being at rehearsal and the two of them being googly-eyed looking at each other,' he said. 'I left for two weeks and came back and they were in love. We were all living in trailers while we were shooting the movie. There were four trailers, and there quickly became three.'

'My relationship with Michelle was something that slowly fell into place. It was a wonderful time. I've been astonished at the profound changes that have happened in my life.' – Heath Ledger

While the romance seems to have blossomed over a couple of weeks, from Heath's perspective he felt it took longer. 'My relationship with Michelle was something that slowly fell into place. We were brought together during this amazing story [*Brokeback Mountain*] and our relationship began to unfold . . . I couldn't [have been] more excited or happier. It was a wonderful time. I've been astonished at the profound changes that have happened in my life.'

Their relationship would go on – like the movie itself – to become one of the defining aspects of Heath Ledger's all-too-short life.

But for now, a crucial period of rehearsal would engage Ledger further. He hadn't auditioned for the movie, much to his relief, but the chance to discuss and develop the characters in a mutually supportive environment had become ever more important to his acting process. 'We all spent time with Ang talking about and rehearsing our characters' stories,' said Heath. 'His attention to detail is microscopic; he doesn't miss a beat. He's a wonderful filmmaker who always seems to know exactly what he wants. He slips into possession of the story he's telling with ease.'

Lee was clear on how he wanted to structure what was really a rather slight tale. 'To make a great romantic story, you need great obstacles. Ennis and Jack are in the American West, which has macho and traditional values. So, everything they feel, they have to keep private. It's precious, and something special that they cannot articulate. That's very dramatic for me.'

The drama of the forbidden relationship got Ledger's creative juices flowing. 'I think most of the emotions or love within Ennis is purely potential,' he said, describing his character's inner depths. 'It's within him and he never really expresses [it]. That's the tragedy of this story. With his wife, his love is slightly manufactured. It's more traditional, but it's not true love. His love for Jack is true as a passionate love, but he hates the way he feels: it's forbidden. Essentially, he's a homophobic male in love with another man. He's very fixed in his ways and he's left lingering in between.'

'I left for two weeks and came back and they were in love.
We were all living in trailers while we were shooting the movie.
There were four trailers, and there quickly became three.'
– Jake Gyllenhaal

Left: *Heath and co-star Michelle Williams relax between takes on the Canadian* Brokeback Mountain *set in 2004.*
Above: *Young couple Ennis (Heath) and Alma (Michelle Williams) enter into a doomed marriage.*

'Ang has a superb understanding of the intimacy
and internal nature of film acting. His attention to detail is
microscopic in pre-production. He trusts you to have given birth to the
instincts, brain and breath of the character, and instead of directing
you, he directs the environment around you to make it believable.'
– Heath Ledger

Lee, Gyllenhaal and Ledger had to determine how far to go in depicting the physical nature of Jack and Ennis's relationship onscreen. 'Clearly, it's pretty challenging material,' Gyllenhaal said, 'but Ang said two men herding sheep was far more sexual than two men having sex on screen.'

For Ledger, the physical moments between the two lead characters were simply narrative milestones. 'There are not actually love scenes for the sake of doing a love scene. There are actually stories within each of those moments. The first moment for Ennis was very poignant because it had to be rough; he had to be fighting it. He was almost ready to punch [Jack]. Once that's all settled, it had to be innate, passionate adrenaline. It just takes over him. There's another moment in the tent where it was really important to show a glimpse of Ennis in a vulnerable state.'

'I think Ennis punishes himself over an uncontrollable need – love. Fear was installed in him at an early age, and so the way he loved disgusted him. He's a walking contradiction.' – Heath Ledger

Ledger was appreciative of his collaborator: 'He was a very brave and talented actor to work with,' while their co-star, veteran character actor Randy Quaid, said, '*Brokeback Mountain* is a courageous choice for both of these actors. They're at a critical phase of their careers, establishing themselves. It's a real credit to them, not only as actors but as people, to take on these roles.'

For his part, Heath saw others' misgivings about the role as a positive reason why he should tackle it. 'I had fear going into it,' he confessed, 'but that was all the more reason to do it; it was exhilarating when I committed. I think Ennis punishes himself over an uncontrollable need – love. Fear was installed in him at an early age, and so the way he loved disgusted him. He's a walking contradiction.'

'Brokeback Mountain is Ennis and Jack's magical place,' explained screenwriter Diana Ossana. 'It's where they fell in love. They never go back there, which may be unconscious on their parts; it's their idyll, and they don't want to spoil it. It's like Jack says, "All we got's Brokeback Mountain."'

Director Ang Lee felt the movie was one of his best efforts, agreeing with Ossana that the theme of the movie and its title location were inextricably tied together. 'The dramatic core is finding Brokeback Mountain. It is elusive and romantic. It is something that you keep wanting to go back to, but probably never will. For Ennis and Jack, it was their taste of love.'

Michelle Williams was impressed by both actors' commitment to the veracity of their characters, no matter how uncomfortable they may have been. 'My hat is off to both of them; Heath was totally supportive, selfless, and helpful.'

And he was equally taken with her talents. 'Michelle's ability to dive deep within her soul never ceased to amaze me. She's a brilliant actress.'

The increasingly frosty relationship that develops between their characters had become completely inverted off-screen, and by the end of the *Brokeback Mountain* shoot, they were inseparable.

Heath takes instruction from director Ang Lee. He described filming Brokeback Mountain *as 'a very lonely experience'.*

5. HIGHS AND LOWS

'I feel like I was very much focusing more on chaos in the past, and now the chaos has kind of washed away and, like anything chaotic, left something beautiful. My life is just working, it's a well-oiled machine at the moment.'
– Heath Ledger

When Heath proceeded to make *Casanova*, it almost seemed like a reaction against the character of Ennis in *Brokeback Mountain*. He'd go from playing a hesitant, guiltily gay man to the reputedly greatest of all heterosexual lovers, in a contemporary retelling of his eighteenth-century legend.

Lasse Hallström, who'd directed such serious dramas as *The Cider House Rules*, *Chocolat* and *The Shipping News*, had to find an actor who could embody all of Casanova's most extraordinary qualities – and then allow them to fall apart in poignant moments of heartbreak. Early on, the search was for an actor in his thirties or forties who could project the feeling of someone who has loved a lot of beautiful women, but is beginning to feel the need to settle down. However, when Hallström encountered the younger Heath Ledger, his approach to the film changed dramatically. 'Heath walked in the room and he was Casanova,' remembered producer Betsy Beers. 'It was one of those amazing things. He was funny, charming and very, very seductive. But he was also elegant and quite vulnerable.'

Heath seemed to possess the mix of dramatic and comedic skills central to the role, and displayed a physical prowess that would prove invaluable. 'Heath is smart, easy-going, captivating and his physical abilities are amazing,' said Hallström.

As for the actor himself, his current criteria for accepting roles was easily met by *Casanova* – but as a piece of fun rather than a serious work of art. 'I loved the script and I've always really admired Lasse as a director so I jumped at the opportunity to work with him,' confirmed Ledger. 'I thought Casanova as he was written in this screenplay would be an incredible amount of fun to play, and of course, I was only too happy to travel to Venice. I understood what type of *Casanova* they wanted to make . . . *Brokeback Mountain* was really hard, so this would be a great way to relax.'

As Casanova, reputedly 'the world's greatest lover', Heath was able to adopt a far more relaxed approach to his performance than he'd employed during the 'torturous' Brokeback Mountain shoot.

Once he committed to the role, Ledger began to research the real-life story of Casanova but decided not to delve too deeply. 'I tackled some of Casanova's journals and autobiography,' he said of his preparatory reading, 'but I didn't want to follow them to a tee. I wanted to keep my portrait of him loose. Particularly after coming off *Brokeback*, which was so serious and lonely and at times torturous, I wanted to come home smiling after work.'

In the part of Francesca, the one woman that Casanova really wants but who resists his allure, Hallström cast Sienna Miller for 'that combination of intelligence, charisma and charm that actually carries the character and makes Casanova's love for her so believable'.

Heath had to wait to wrap *Brokeback Mountain*, in August 2004, before he could join the cast and crew of *Casanova*, who had convened a month earlier. 'It was critical for Lasse to shoot in Venice because there is no place else on Earth like it – and Casanova and Venice are inextricably linked,' said producer Mark Gordon. 'While it was complicated logistically, Venice is a major character in *Casanova*.'

It certainly provided inspiration for Ledger. 'It was an absolute dream. It was like spending four months in the most amazing museum.'

'Heath walked in the room and he was Casanova. It was one of those amazing things. He was funny, charming and very, very seductive. But he was also elegant and quite vulnerable.' – *Casanova* producer Betsy Beers

Academy Award-winning costume designer Jenny Beavan wanted Casanova's outfits to befit a man of his reputation, without turning him into a dandy. His look would be elegant but simple. 'This is a comedy so our Casanova is not like the tortured Fellini version, for example,' she said. 'When our Casanova falls in love with Francesca, it's for real, but he's also a near-mythical character so we played with those lines. Heath really took to it and loved the heels and lace, and in a way I think he felt that his costumes were a refuge. Heath [had] also studied modern dance so he moves well and makes the clothes look wonderful.'

'It was a vacation really,' said Heath of his time on *Casanova*. 'I've never spent this much time in Venice and it ended up being a four-and-a-half-month guided tour. Every day we ended up being taken to the most beautiful parts of Venice to shoot. *Brokeback Mountain* and *Casanova* complemented each other. [Making] *Brokeback* was excruciating and *Casanova* was drinking wine and eating pasta, it was like a holiday. It's not meant to be the definitive, historical take on Casanova, but rather a romantic comedy.'

Having re-engaged his enthusiasm for acting through the stimulus of professional challenge, at the beginning of 2005 Heath explained why he'd stuck with it, after harbouring thoughts of dropping out. 'It's escapism, an extension of my curiosity,' he stated. 'I love the striving, the process of being part of something bigger than me, because it forces me to examine myself.'

But, still, he was increasingly of the opinion that acting was actually a rather

Heath spent four months on location in Venice while filming tongue-in-cheek
period romp Casanova *(2005). 'It was an absolute dream' said the actor.*

'It was an opportunity not to take acting too seriously . . . Essentially we were borrowing his name and his legend and just having fun with it.'
– Heath Ledger

'I thought Casanova as he was written in this screenplay
would be an incredible amount of fun to play, and of course,
I was only too happy to travel to Venice.'
– Heath Ledger

Left and above: *Casanova (Heath) devotes himself to the task of wooing the reluctant Francesca (Sienna Miller) amidst the pomp and revelry of eighteenth-century Venice.*

silly profession. 'That's a thought I cannot have in the middle of a scene. The second I realise what I'm really doing – I'm a glorified monkey dressed up in an outfit – it's like, "What are you doing, Heath? Oh, go home."'

Ledger was not content to rest on his laurels. He was driven, restless, always looking for a new challenge, even as he coped with the fallout from his most recent character. 'I still have far to go. That's what this year was about, pushing myself . . . I don't ever want to consider myself a good actor, because, well, I think I'm not. It allows you to be lazy if you start to think you're "hot". I'm not as good as I want to be. I don't think I'll ever be as good as I want to be, but I'll keep striving for it.'

While Michelle and Heath weren't contemplating marriage, the thought of having children seems to have come up fairly quickly. 'Very early in our relationship, we talked about having babies together,' Heath acknowledged. 'I always knew I'd be a young father.'

The questions of Ledger's emotional maturity that so seemed to trouble Naomi Watts didn't seem to be a problem for Williams. Perhaps their similarity in ages, and the fact that they'd both been actors since they were young teenagers made them more compatible. In some respects, Ledger suggested that the decision to have a child was something they didn't consciously decide upon. 'We just fell very deeply into one another's arms. Our bodies definitely made those decisions for us. I mean, the second you acknowledge [having a child] as a possibility, the body just inevitably hits a switch and it happens.'

**'Brokeback Mountain and Casanova complemented each other. Making Brokeback was excruciating and Casanova was drinking wine and eating pasta, it was like a holiday.'
– Heath Ledger**

The pair conceived on a trip outside Sydney, in a resort called Byron Bay, a place populated by surfers and travellers seeking enlightenment or spiritual development. 'It's very romantic,' said Heath of the Bay. 'It's very spiritual. There are a lot of hippies out there.'

With the pregnancy confirmed shortly before Ledger began work on shooting his next film, *Candy*, he was already looking forward to the new addition to his life. 'I can't wait to meet my child. We've been preparing,' he said. 'We're both fit and happy and healthy; that's all you can ask for.'

Looking after Williams during this period, Ledger was able to indulge one of his neglected hobbies: cooking. 'Italian is my forte. I'm into hand-making pasta now, hand-making gnocchi and fettuccini. There's flour everywhere in my kitchen. I like making a mess. Michelle does, too. She cooks as well. She's very good.' So proud was the father-to-be that he was keen to promenade with his partner, announcing their pregnant status to the world. 'I love walking around with Michelle, beautifully pregnant, and watching the other mothers acknowledge her; they always kind of throw a wink or a little smile or a nod of encouragement.'

Films in which the lead character suffers from an affliction or an addiction are often attractive to ambitious actors as they provide the opportunity for a dramatic showcase; a chance to show off rarely afforded when playing more 'ordinary' parts. It was partly with this in mind that Heath Ledger opted to follow the acclaimed double whammy of *Brokeback Mountain* and *Casanova* with the role of drug-addicted would-be poet Dan in *Candy*. 'I had no real desire to play a junkie,' he said, 'but love is very important in my life and it's something I am always interested to find within a story. I like it to be smuggled [in] or disguised in other backdrops.'

'I don't ever want to consider myself a good actor, because, well, I think I'm not. It allows you to be lazy if you start to think you're "hot". I'm not as good as I want to be. I don't think I'll ever be as good as I want to be, but I'll keep striving for it.'
– Heath Ledger

The movie, directed by experienced theatre director Neil Armfield, was based on Luke Davies's 1997 Australian bestselling novel. Abbie Cornish was cast in the title role of Candy, a young painter and the object of Dan's romantic obsession. Caught up in each other, the pair find themselves immersed in the hedonistic pleasures of heroin use, only for their lives to turn sour as the realities and humiliations of addiction kick in. Despite being younger than the character in the novel, Cornish was the director's first choice for the role of Candy. However, the idea of casting Heath Ledger as Dan, suggested by the novel's author, was not as straightforward. Thinking of Ledger as the comedy-heroic type from *A Knight's Tale*, the image the actor had been working so hard to overcome, Armfield was reluctant to cast him initially. '[Dan is] a man spun around and dazzled by the beauty of the world,' explained Armfield, who also saw his lead character as someone who was 'prepared to allow his partner the humiliation of selling herself in order to fuel their addiction. Heath's natural energy is heroic. I thought we needed someone grubbier or edgier for Dan.'

The casting process had taken place before Ledger's *Brokeback Mountain* performance was seen, so Armfield was not aware of the range and versatility that Ledger was in the process of developing. There was one performance, however, that gave a glimpse of what Heath was capable of. It was a viewing of *Monster's Ball* that caused Armfield to give the young actor more serious consideration. He took time out to travel to Prague, where Ledger was then shooting *The Brothers Grimm*, to meet with the actor and discuss the role in *Candy*. 'I guess it's a love triangle,' Ledger recognised, 'between them and the drug. I think they're just kind of intertwined. I think we were all telling ourselves that it was more a love story than a story of heroin.'

Soon, the subject that Ledger dreaded raised its head: an audition. For Armfield, this wasn't so much to see what Ledger would do with the part, as he was more concerned with establishing what kind of chemistry – if any – his two potential leads might have. 'I realised that there was a very precise working energy between them, and a chemistry,' Armfield said, relieved. 'It was fantastic. Abbie and Heath knew that as a lead in a film you have to take responsibility for your own centre, and they both did that quite magnificently.'

Ledger was happy to finally be making a film in Australia once again, following his good experiences on *Ned Kelly*. 'I'm constantly looking for material in Australia,' he said. 'It's so liberating to perform without an accent. It gave me a sense of freedom, being able to mumble, to breathe in my own accent. I was able to improvise more freely. This, and the faith I had in the film, that it was going to be a good story to tell, and my curiosity to see what Neil Armfield would do with it, drew me back to Australia.'

As for the gloomy subject matter of the film, after *Casanova* Ledger felt ready to indulge his dark side again. 'I had the energy to be dark again, because I'd been in bloody Venice drinking too much wine and eating. I do think that drugs and alcohol have been glorified and mythologised. Creation [as in Dan's poetry and Candy's paintings] comes from your mind and it's hard to create when you're drugged out. I'm sure drugs and alcohol could inspire new thoughts, but it's certainly not something that I use as a tool or a mechanism to create.'

'We just fell very deeply into one another's arms. Our bodies definitely made those decisions for us.' – Heath Ledger on Michelle's pregnancy

High on the agenda before filming for both actors was a period of intense research. The pair felt the need to immerse themselves in the reality of the local drug culture in order to capture it on film and in their performances. 'Abbie and I went to the Narcotics Users Association in Sydney, where we met a guy who'd been addicted to heroin for twenty years,' Ledger declared. Part of their concern was simply about the practical issues of how addicts behave. 'He took us through the steps of how to shoot up. He took a prosthetic arm with veins and blood bags and showed us how to find the vein and the angle to slip the needle in. They're designed to teach nurses how to find veins, but they have one here to teach kids how to inject safely. We'd grabbed a video camera and filmed it. I gave the DVD to [co-star] Geoffrey Rush, one to the Art Department and one to Neil, as reference.'

Ledger's own, according to him rather limited, drug experiences were also useful in informing his performance. 'I've smoked pot before, and I know what it feels like to be high,' he admitted. 'I've never been addicted to anything other than cigarettes, although that's quite an addiction. With heroin there's so many television documentaries, shows, movies and books, [that] you feel you know how they do it, even if you've never been anywhere near it.'

The author of the original novel had some drug wisdom to impart to Ledger. 'Luke Davies was on set all the time and was there to say things that we wouldn't know, like "When you're stoned on heroin, your eyes aren't like that, but your eyebrows are up."' Davies even put in an on-screen cameo appearance as the milkman who, memorably, hands the young lovers free cartons of milk in the pre-dawn dark.

Davies would later write of the tender scenes he witnessed between Heath and the newly-pregnant Michelle before filming had begun in earnest. 'He seemed, at times, quite literally beside himself with love for her, unable to contain his

If love is the drug. Poet Dan (Heath) and art student Candy (Abbie Cornish) find themselves addicted to heroin – and each other – in the dark and poignant Candy *(2006).*

'I do think that drugs and alcohol have been glorified and mythologised. I'm sure drugs and alcohol could inspire new thoughts, but it's certainly not something that I use as a tool or a mechanism to create.'
– Heath Ledger

excitement. I remember one night during preproduction, in an almost empty nightclub in Kings Cross, watching him sweep her to her feet and swirl her around an empty dance floor, much to the relief of a bored DJ. It was a completely private moment; he wasn't doing it for the benefit of others, for those of us settling into our seats or buying a round. He just wanted to dance with Michelle. One almost felt the need to avert one's eyes, and yet it was oddly compelling: that pure joy again.'

Production on *Candy* began on 17 March 2005 and continued over seven weeks entirely on location in Sydney's Inner West, the Eastern Suburbs and in regional New South Wales. 'Neil wanted to do a lot of rehearsal because he had an extensive theatre background,' recalled Ledger of the beginning of filming. 'Abbie and I were the naughty kids in class who sat in the back. We didn't want to give too much. It was slightly superstitious of us both. We didn't want to capture our performance in rehearsal. We were nervous about it because we were not sure we could repeat it in the shoot. Neil backed down and let us work in our own patterns.'

Ledger saw his role as that of the lead protagonist, the one who leads Candy astray as both fall deeper into an addiction they initially see as an extension of their passionate romance. 'When you first meet Dan in the film he's knee deep in addiction. He's a regular user of heroin and a poet. He looks at drug use as poetic and romantic. Candy's curiosity towards drugs is born through him. He's attracted by the way she wants to dive into his world, to share his experience. Heroin ends up binding the two of them together, and destroying them as a couple. They go to hell and back. *Candy* is also the story of their rebirth.'

'I've smoked pot before, and I know what it feels like to be high. I've never been addicted to anything other than cigarettes, although that's quite an addiction.'
– Heath Ledger

One challenge the pair faced was filming the numerous love scenes the film required. According to Heath, filming such scenes is never as easy as audiences might think. 'There is nothing attractive about that process, even if [the other actor] is an attractive person. There's nothing organic about it. The grips, gaffers and focus pullers are looking at your butt. It's so nerve-wracking and very uncomfortable.'

Some of Heath's realistic work on *Candy* hit the cutting-room floor. 'I did one scene they didn't end up using. It was near the end of the movie when I inject again [after being clean]. There was a shot that we had, a tight shot of my arm, and I slipped the needle in and pulled back until you saw the blood, and then they went off it onto my face. I actually injected. It had coloured water and sugar in it to make it look watery brown. Then we found out that was the difference between an M rating [for 'Mature' in Australia, equivalent to an R in the US and an 18 in the UK] and an R, due to the penetration [of the needle]. When it looked like it was going in and it didn't really go in, that was okay.'

The filming of one scene in particular caused Heath notable difficulties, made all the more problematic by his and Michelle's personal circumstances. The script called for a miscarriage, in which Abbie Cornish's Candy gives birth to a stillborn

After the 'paid holiday' that constituted his work on Casanova,
Heath was prepared to tackle Candy's *bleak and demanding subject matter.*

baby. Heath feared by participating he might be tempting fate with regard to Michelle's own pregnancy. It was purely superstition, but the actor felt it quite strongly. 'It was terrible shooting that [scene],' he admitted. 'We'd found out a month earlier that we were having a baby. I don't usually get disturbed by scenes, but that was really tough. In between takes I was running off and calling Michelle, telling her I loved her. I didn't want to jinx my own personal life with this scene.'

Ledger even took it upon himself to try to persuade the director that the scene didn't have to be shown. 'I protested a lot about it. I would have liked it to be more suggested than graphic. You do actually see a lot less on film than what was shot, but it was still horrible. This little prosthetic baby, all bloody, looked so real. It was not nice. I didn't want to jinx our own pregnancy, having to hold a little prosthetic, bloody dead baby in my hands. It was definitely difficult to shoot.'

The scene was shot, and sensitively edited by director Neil Armfield in the finished film. Ledger quickly moved on from it, looking forward to the changes about to happen in his life.

But there was an increasingly serious problem in Heath and Michelle's life which escalated during filming, when Heath's already pronounced difficulties with the Australian media were to take an ugly turn during the final days of the *Candy* shoot.

'When they kind of spy in on you and you're trying to bathe out in the sun, and you're with your girlfriend and your friends and your family – it actually feels like you're getting a slap across the face.' – Heath Ledger

He had previously been lambasted for eating an orange during a television interview with journalist Katherine Tulich of Australia's Seven Network show *Sunrise*. The broadcast item brought a storm of protest from viewers (and was available for many around the world to see thanks to the Internet), with Ledger condemned as a rude and inconsiderate interviewee. Tulich felt that the actor was simply not focused on the job at hand, feeling he was disinterested in talking about the movie. 'I didn't actually ask him any hard questions,' she said. 'It was a short interview and no matter what I did, I couldn't get his attention away from the orange.'

'It was the worst thing I could have done,' Ledger admitted, looking back on the incident. 'When it was aired, on the morning TV show, they had people calling in asking, "Who does he think he is? He's not Nicole Kidman. He should get off his high horse." Then, the next day, they had oranges on the show and were chucking them around, saying I could stick an orange up my . . . you know what.'

The actor realised he'd scored a PR own-goal with his conduct and issued an apology, blaming his own inexperience and the lack of a lunch break for his conduct. 'It was one of about 60 television interviews I completed in that sitting and it sounds like you landed the dud,' he said in a public message to Tulich. 'I remember peeling that orange and eating it through an interview. In hindsight it probably wasn't a polite thing to do. I was just hungry and a little dehydrated. I'm just figuring out how to play this "game". I'm not sure I put thought into how I

Heath soaks up some rays on the beach near his Sydney home.

want to be perceived and how I come across. I've never really concentrated on that. All my effort goes in between the time of action and cut.'

The forthright apology seemed to do the trick. 'I had them read it out on air. I went from zero to hero,' said Heath, happy to have repaired the damage. 'The audience reaction was, "That nice Heath must have a good family, and he is well brought up. We love him – isn't he a great actor?" Australians are the world's greatest at cutting you down to size, and I'd better not forget it. I just have to remember not to take myself too seriously.'

This fractious relationship with the Australian media – particularly an aggressive contingent of Sydney-based photographers – had cast a shadow over Heath and Michelle's time there. 'When poor Michelle wants to go out, she ends up just turning around and taking the car straight home, almost in tears, because she has these cars following her,' Heath said, concluding: 'I didn't want to raise a child under those conditions.'

The penultimate night of filming for *Candy* witnessed an event whose eventual outcome directly influenced the couple's decision to sell their Sydney home and leave Australia indefinitely.

'When it's true love, it feels like something you're rekindling, as if you've met the person before.' – Heath Ledger

'We were doing a scene on the street in Newtown and a small crowd had gathered to watch,' recalled director Neil Armfield. 'It had been a hard day and we were desperately short of time and were covering the scene in a single choreographed shot. We were on our third – and best – take, and from the crowd came the flash of a camera, a man called out "flash" and walked away fast up the street. The take was ruined.

'In the confusion – had a lamp blown? – nobody knew what had happened except Heath. He bolted up the street after the photographer – Guy Finlay – shouting abuse. Finlay screamed "I'll see you at home, Ledger!" It was only Heath who had the speed and courage of reaction. I was ashamed to have stood there in stunned incomprehension. I wish I'd chased him too. I wish I'd smashed his camera.' As Heath gave chase, Guy Finlay stumbled and fell to the ground. He would later inform the police that he had been assaulted by Ledger, and spread rumours that Heath had spat at him and other photographers on the *Candy* set, a vehemently denied accusation that was to haunt the increasingly media-wary actor for years to come.

One anti-paparazzi initiative that Heath did admit to and freely indulged in during this period was egg-throwing. 'I've thrown an egg,' he said. 'Not at them, just kind of next to them so it splatters up against them. That's how pathetic it is. That's what we're reduced to. You can't actually stand up and slap them. When they kind of spy in on you and you're trying to bathe out in the sun, and you're with your girlfriend and your friends and your family – it actually feels like you're getting a slap across the face. And we can't physically stand up and hit them back, of course, it would be rude and against the law. So you just get an egg.' Even these light-hearted attempts at retaliation,

Heath and Michelle take a beer at sunset.

however, ultimately served to do no more than give the paparazzi what they wanted: a reaction that could be photographed and sold.

Media intrusions and the stress Heath had increasingly come to associate with his Australian base notwith-standing, *Candy* wrapped in May 2005, and Ledger was happy to be able to indulge two of his favourite pastimes that he'd had to put on hold for the duration in order to achieve an appropriately pallid junkie's physique. 'I had to stay out of the sun and I tried to eat less,' he declared. Now sunshine and feasting awaited.

Despite Heath's serious difficulties with the media during the shoot, when *Candy* was released a year later, in May 2006 in Australia, October and November in the US and the UK, his performance received much critical acclaim. *Variety*'s Russell Edwards saw *Candy* as 'a mostly bitter, but occasionally sweet, concoction'. According to the review, the film 'belongs to Heath Ledger . . . Ledger convincingly adds to his repertoire with a warm depiction of the charmingly co-dependent Dan who both fuels and fears the addiction of his girlfriend.' Writing in The *Los Angeles Times*, Carina Chocano said of *Candy*: '[It's] a love story about a boy, a girl and a drug. Much of the credit goes to Ledger [who] exerts a sideways pull as the loving but toxic lost boy who lures Candy away from her safe but stifling milieu.' In the *San Francisco Chronicle*, Ruthe Stein observed that 'The energy Ledger projects as Dan becomes scary when fuelled by heroin. Ledger is mesmerising in a scene where Dan pulls off a white-collar crime by going to a bank with a stolen ID and charming a cashier into giving him more than $2,000. Hyped up, he keeps repeating to himself, "I'm rolling," like a mantra.' The *Village Voice* noted that 'Ledger, long-haired and so soft-looking you'd think he was shot slightly out of focus, is the movie's real eye candy,' while the *Chicago Tribune* summed Ledger up as 'a chameleon-like ace. Ledger is alive and awake and interesting every minute of *Candy*. His performance betrays not a speck of vanity or evident calculation; it's all nerve endings and momentary thrills and emotional need. The rest of the film isn't up to his level.'

Even with such high praise for Heath, the film was regarded as an 'art movie' by American theatres, due to its dealing with drugs and being Australian, and *Candy* opened on only one screen in November 2006. The initial weekend box office was $3,646, ending in a total US take of just $44,720 by February 2007, having never played on more than eight screens nationwide in any one week.

Following their departure from Sydney, Heath, Michelle, and the imminent arrival returned to New York (where Williams had been based before meeting Ledger) and purchased a $4.5 million, four-storey Brownstone in Brooklyn's affluent and village-like Boerum Hill. 'Moving to Brooklyn [one of the five boroughs of New York City] is the greatest decision I ever made,' Heath claimed. 'I really appreciate Brooklyn because, quite frankly, no one gives a shit [about who I am] there. Sydney is scaring me at the moment. I feel like the paparazzi are going to kick me out of that city. I do not feel like living there any more. It's a shame, because I absolutely love it. Unfortunately, that's keeping me away from Australia.'

Being away from Hollywood allowed him some kind of normalcy, even privacy, despite his new status as a bona fide star. 'The best thing about Brooklyn is it's removed. I just live a really normal life. I lug my laundry down to the laundromat. I keep the house nice and tidy and clean. I go shopping at the supermarket. I cook. I commute on the train back and forth, in and out of town. I sit and I observe all these people around me, all these lives and these stories. It's really stimulating. I feel like I'm really living for the first time. It's wonderful.'

Ledger may have escaped the attentions of the paparazzi for a while, but in 2005 they would continue to be a major issue for him and Michelle. Still, he regarded himself as extremely lucky to have met her. 'Michelle and I are forever in debt to Ang [Lee], in a much smaller sense for giving us this movie, but on a grander scale for kind of putting us together.'

'I will never be satisfied with my position in this industry. I never want to be. You have to be a particular type of person to be self-satisfied. I am just not that type. I do not want to be settled on one opinion, one path and one way of life. I want to evolve, expand and go deeper within myself.' – Heath Ledger

This time, despite all his prior relationships, he felt that he had something different. 'When it's true love, it feels like something you're rekindling,' the actor claimed. '[It's] as if you've met the person before. She's my soul mate and we couldn't love each other any more than we do already. We're like two peas in a pod.'

Off-screen, their story was as different from the two characters that had brought them together as could be imagined. 'I think it would've been boring if we were in love on screen,' Heath claimed, 'it would've been easy and obvious. We were working against the odds! It was out of our control, it was just something very beautiful and deep. The whole thing was astonishing. My relationship with Michelle was something that slowly fell into place. Falling in love with her had nothing to do with the environment or the subject matter of [*Brokeback Mountain*].'

Michelle reflected on how their relationship was born out of playing characters in emotional turmoil. 'Maybe it was that thing of finding order in chaos . . . There were so many unknowns during the day while we were working, that we managed to find a little bit of order in the off-set time.'

For the first time, Heath felt like he was finding peace both professionally and in his personal life. Everything was coming together at last, after years of failed relationships and frustration at the quality of his work. 'It just seems to me that when you clean your act up and start ironing out kinks in your life, whether professional or social, synchronicity follows. I feel like I was very much focusing more on chaos in the past, and now the chaos has kind of washed away and, like anything chaotic, left something beautiful. My life is just working, it's a well-oiled machine at the moment.'

Adding to his tattoos while in New York, Heath had 'Old Man River' inscribed on his arm over where Michelle had written the words in ink. It joined 'KAOS' – the acronym formed from his mother's and sisters' names – and a Canadian maple leaf on his right hand. 'It's not the song,' he explained of 'Old Man River'. 'It's got

a few meanings, but I'll tell you one. It feels so eternal, just those words. And I feel like I'm at a time in my life now where I'm paddling down that river. I'm on my way and life is about to speed up. Maybe I should slow down and appreciate it.'

Matilda Rose Ledger was born on 28 October 2005, weighing in at 2.83kg. The child's godparents were Ledger's *Brokeback Mountain* co-star Jake Gyllenhaal and Williams's *Dawson's Creek* cast-mate Busy Phillips. Gyllenhaal wryly noted, 'Heath and I made out, but Heath and Michelle had the baby.'

New mother Michelle Williams claimed she knew the exact minute she decided to name her daughter Matilda. It was during a mundane trip on a New York subway. 'I came up with it on the subway one day,' she said. 'It just fell from the sky and into my head. I love, absolutely love, the Roald Dahl book *Matilda*. I didn't think about it at the time, but then afterwards, I was like, "Yeah, that's the girl I want my daughter to be. She'll read lots of books and make things move with her eyes. Yes, that'll be my daughter, for sure."'

Ang Lee, whose exacting casting process had brought Williams and Ledger together, philosophically observed of little Matilda: 'The baby keeps staring at me. Michelle said she doesn't usually stare at people like that. I said maybe she remembers I am the reason she came into existence.'

Following the birth, Ledger's Brooklyn neighbours – who'd been giving the starry couple plenty of personal space, much to Heath's relief – started turning up with casserole dishes. 'It was very sweet,' the shy actor acknowledged. Again, his urge to cook overcame him. 'I made a big feast for them, [and] we got to know each other.' Heath would cement these newfound friendships by offering his neighbours tickets to *Brokeback Mountain*'s star-studded New York premiere.

Above: The elegant Brownstone house Heath and Michelle purchased in Brooklyn's Boerum Hill.
Right: Heath and a visibly pregnant Michelle attend the Los Angeles premiere of The Brothers Grimm.

'I can't wait to meet my child. We've been preparing. We're both fit and happy and healthy; that's all you can ask for.' – Heath Ledger

Ledger knew things were going to be different now, both personally and professionally. Starting a family, Heath conceded, 'changes the person you are', but he quickly added, 'I didn't immediately get an urge to be a voice in an animated film. Fatherhood is what I've always wanted. It definitely exceeds my expectations, but I was always expecting it – and a lot from it. It's marvellous,' he said, adding that he hoped to have six children eventually. 'It is wonderful to feel the profound changes it will make in my life and my beliefs. There are no plans for marriage, yet, but I could not be more excited or happier.'

'The best thing about Brooklyn is it's removed. I just live a really normal life. I cook. I commute on the train back and forth. I sit and I observe all these people around me, all these lives and these stories. It's really stimulating. I feel like I'm really living for the first time. It's wonderful.' – Heath Ledger

Waking every morning to cater to the needs of the new member of the family was something that came naturally to Heath. 'Just waking up every morning to that smile brightens your day, it really does. I've been able to cook and clean and be Michelle's chauffeur and keep her comfortable and relaxed. We had a wonderful pregnancy and a wonderful birth and we equally supported each other through this.'

It was a new role for Ledger, but one he tackled more enthusiastically than he had any other. 'I'm Mr. Mom! Every day I wake up and prepare two breakfasts: I get [Michelle] granola and cook her an egg, I clean the dishes, and then I'm cooking lunch. Later, I go out to the market and get fresh produce for dinner, and then I cook that. I love my new job.'

Naturally, as with all new parents, there were difficulties, but in his joy at becoming a father, Ledger was even prepared to live with the negatives. 'Even the exhaustion from lack of sleep – it's just a pleasure to have this form of exhaustion. I'm up at 5:30am or 6am every morning, and in bed at 9pm. The one thing I realised is that, before Matilda, we were just sleeping in too long. We were missing out on so much of the day. I get much more done now; I feel more focused. I actually need to go to bed at 9pm now, I feel it in my bones.' With his new responsibilities, Ledger was hardly the hard-partying young actor that many would expect someone in his professional position to be at his age (and as he would later be portrayed after his death).

Professionally, Ledger decided to take a break from making films, committing to an eighteen-month period of parental leave. After *Candy*, his focus was on his home life and his two girls. 'We've just been living in Brooklyn and really committing our time to Matilda,' he said of himself and Michelle. 'We've just been letting it consume us. We wanted to distance ourselves [from the business], and we couldn't think of anything better to do than wake up to play with our child. That's the biggest gift this industry has given us; the ability to do that.'

The down time was great for Heath: he was able to let go of many of the anxieties that performing in films generally caused him. There was no question of struggling to perform, or uncertainty about whether he was performing his role properly. He had instant gratification every day in the form of his wife and child's

Jake Gyllenhaal, Heath, Michelle, and Ang Lee celebrate the success of Brokeback Mountain *at the 2006 Bafta Awards in London.*

'Heath and I made out, but Heath and Michelle had the baby.' – Jake Gyllenhaal

happiness. Choosing his roles carefully had become Ledger's new approach to work, from *Brokeback Mountain* through to *Candy*, but now he had even more incentive not to commit to a film unless something about it really captured him or challenged him. 'Matilda is just awesome,' Heath said of his daughter. 'Being a father has helped me become even more selective now with work because for me to go away from home for a day, let alone five, is tough.'

'I'm just so comfortable right now,' the contented actor continued. '[I'm] really relaxed. I find I'm liking myself more for it. I'm learning more about myself. I have a lot more time to think. When you do get a slice of freedom, you do something with it. If you're going to watch a movie, you make sure it's a good one. You get to siphon out the crap.'

'Siphoning out the crap' would become Heath's new mantra, as he knew time with his wife and daughter was precious. 'She's such an awesome, beautiful little girl that Michelle and I hate spending five minutes away from her, never mind five months [on a movie], so it has to be really, really worth it.'

The relentless press schedules that marked the run-up to the release of

Casanova and *Brokeback Mountain* began only six weeks after Matilda's birth. And after a while the professional pressure on Ledger – and on Williams – to return to work grew. As during his time with Naomi Watts, the pair had to work out a method whereby they could both work. The added complication was having a third person in the relationship who also had to be looked after. 'When Michelle is working, I'm the nanny, and when I'm working, Michelle's the nanny,' said Heath of their family arrangements. 'When she was working [in LA], I was in a hotel room and it was really hard. Whether we like it or not, we go in and out of LA all the time. We found a one-bedroom tree-house [once owned by Ellen DeGeneres] up in the hills out there. It's just a place to drop our bags.'

Ledger was concerned to keep his professional ambitions and needs under control. 'We've tried to cater our lives and our professional lives towards not getting to that place,' said Ledger, referring to some other actors' tendency to become profligate and make huge demands. 'I don't need to own a skyscraper and I don't need to fly my own jet. I don't need all those things, so therefore I don't need to get myself in that position, trapped within my own empire. [There] is a choice. You choose to get there.'

'It is wonderful to feel the profound changes it will make in my life and my beliefs.' – Heath Ledger on fatherhood

Despite having Matilda to look after, Heath realised that he had to be equally attentive to Michelle. The pair couldn't lose sight of their own relationship, and they found their attitude to things around them changing. 'Michelle and I really appreciate small spaces now,' said Ledger. 'Our lives feel smaller. We're far away from everything else. It helps us survive. I couldn't ask for better timing in my life. Any hype or excitement around work doesn't mean anything. Having this child has taken any pressure off my shoulders in terms of what people think of the movies. It doesn't matter. Our love for each other grows. We had a really good relationship [before Matilda] and we still love, respect and are patient with each other. Even with all the new demands, pressures and challenges we still work really well together and it doesn't break us.'

Even before *Brokeback Mountain*'s ecstatic critical reception and the film's subsequent irreversible impact (for both good and bad) upon his career and personal life, Heath recognised that: 'The movie's already exceeded any expectations I had. I think pleasing Annie Proulx, the writer, and getting her nod of approval was the biggest success for me, for us.'

Even so, at a private screening of the film attended by Heath and Williams upon completion of the post-production process, he remained insistently sceptical about his on-screen achievement. 'I understood that it flowed, that it was *presented* well,' he claimed. 'But whether it was good, whether it was bad – we walked out not knowing what we'd just watched.'

Annie Proulx, for one, was particularly forthcoming in her praise for Ledger's cinematic interpretation of the character she had created eight years previously. 'Heath Ledger erased the image I had when I wrote it,' said the Pulitzer Prize-

Heath and a nine-month-old Matilda take time out during a shopping trip in Brooklyn.

Heath signs autographs for fans at the 2005 Venice Film Festival.

'Sydney is scaring me at the moment. I feel like the paparazzi are going to kick me out of that city. I do not feel like living there any more. It's a shame, because I absolutely love it. Unfortunately, that's keeping me away from Australia.' – Heath Ledger

winner. 'He was so visceral. How did this actor get inside my head so well? He understood more about the character than I did. This isn't nice for a 70-year-old woman to say, but it was a skullfuck.'

Casanova was one of three movies starring Heath Ledger that premiered at the 62nd Venice Film Festival in September 2005, alongside *The Brothers Grimm* and *Brokeback Mountain*. The trio of films served as an apt representation of his newfound diversity, and Ledger emerged as the most talked-about and press-courted actor in attendance.

Heath's turn as *Casanova* was a showy performance that drew much critical attention (especially following recent acclaim for *Brokeback Mountain*), despite mixed reviews. Kevin Thomas in the *Los Angeles Times* wrote that each of his two most recent characters was a remarkable stretch for the actor, concluding he was 'equally engaging and convincing in both roles'. A. O. Scott in the *New York Times* felt, 'Ledger's status as the pansexual art-house heartthrob of the season will only be enhanced by this nimble performance.' Wesley Morris, in the *Boston Globe*, observed how, in *Casanova*, 'Ledger brings a terrific blend of slyness and virility to the role of an unstoppable, bewigged libertine whose conquests include an entire nunnery.' Jan Stuart in *Newsday* suggested a more calculated career plan than Ledger would ever admit to: 'One can't help but feel the nudging hand of an agent behind his back-to-back roles in *Brokeback Mountain* and *Casanova*. "Heath, baby, do all the depressed gay cowboys you want. But you gotta get back to your straight roots or there will be no *Brokeback 2*. Here, read this. This guy is a very famous heterosexual. He goes through women like six-packs. He sleeps with nuns. But he's got class."'

When *Casanova* opened in the US on Christmas Day 2005, it was only on a limited run of 37 screens. The opening weekend box office take amounted to just $560,000, although the total gross for what many would regard as an 'art movie' was a relatively healthy $11.3 million. (It also debuted during *Brokeback Mountain*'s fourth week on release, with the 'gay western' taking $4.8 million that week, up 61 per cent from the previous week.)

Heath and Michelle are sprayed with water-pistols by vengeful paparazzi at Brokeback Mountain's *Sydney premiere.*

More important was the psychological boost that both films gave Ledger. 'My only ambition was to improve myself,' he said of his most recent roles. 'I will never be satisfied with my position in this industry. I never want to be. You have to be a particular type of person to be self-satisfied. I am just not that type. I do not want to be settled on one opinion, one path and one way of life. I want to evolve, expand and go deeper within myself.'

The awards for *Brokeback Mountain* came thick and fast. The film won Ang Lee the coveted Golden Lion at Venice. The Los Angeles Film Critics named it as best picture, with Ledger as runner-up for Best Actor (losing to Philip Seymour Hoffman in *Capote*). The film then won Best Picture, Actor (for Ledger) and Director awards from the New York Film Critics Circle, and two more (Best Director and Best Supporting Actor, for Jake Gyllenhaal) from the National Board of Review.

In January 2006, Heath and Michelle returned to Sydney for *Brokeback Mountain*'s Australian premiere. What should have been a triumphant homecoming for Ledger was once again marred by the efforts of the paparazzi, in this case a trio led by Guy Finlay – the photographer who had made it his personal mission to antagonise Ledger on the *Candy* set all those months previously. As Heath and

'Australians are the world's greatest at cutting you down to size, and I'd better not forget it. I just have to remember not to take myself too seriously.' – Heath Ledger

The luxurious beachside home (fifth from left, middle row) in Sydney that Heath sold due to ongoing problems with the Australian paparazzi.

Michelle walked down the red carpet, Finlay and his cohorts sprayed the couple with water pistols in supposed revenge for Ledger's 'spitting'. Heath subsequently had to introduce the film soaked to the skin. 'That broke my heart,' he lamented. 'They obviously wanted me to punch and swear at them, looking [like] a big bad idiot, but I was crushed. I had to introduce the film, but I could barely speak. I went straight home to Bronte, got into the bathroom and broke down.' Afterwards, he made a tearful phone call to his father. 'Heath had to go into the cinema and introduce the film soaking wet,' Kim Ledger would later tell the *Sydney Daily Telegraph*. 'He cried all night. He rang me and said, "Dad, that's it. Sell the house."'

Concerned by the potential outcome of such an impulsive decision, Kim asked Heath to think it over for 48 hours. 'Two days later he rang me back and said, "Dad, it has been 47 hours and 57 minutes. Sell the house."'

During those 48 hours, Heath and Michelle had found themselves besieged by photographers, journalists and TV crews who were summoned to their house by Guy Finlay under the pretext of him publicly apologising to Michelle for the water-pistol incident. However, the would-be apology still came with the insistence that Heath needed to be 'taught a lesson'.

'We were like prisoners in our own house; our own goldfish bowl, it turned out,' Heath said. 'I'd installed dark reflective glass on the balconies and windows, but they had special lenses to shoot pictures of us through the glass.'

This was to be the last in a very long line of final straws. 'I felt so stressed and disheartened. I wanted Michelle to love Australia, but we couldn't live like that.'

The Sydney house was sold for £2.5 million two months later. Heath, Michelle and Matilda flew back to America, and one of Heath's primary ties with his home country was severed.

Brokeback Mountain continued to garner an excess of awards and critical acclaim in the ensuing months, but the focus of the awards season inevitably shifted towards the Oscars. It was nominated for a total of eight Academy Awards, including Best Picture, Best Actor (Ledger), Best Supporting Actor (Jake Gyllenhaal) and Best Supporting Actress (Michelle Williams), alongside Ang Lee for Best Director.

'My personal life is where all the transition is happening, having a child. It completely outweighs any excitement in my career. It pulls this rug of hype out from under my feet and keeps me grounded.' – Heath Ledger

It was 5:30am and the tail-end of a long night spent with a wakeful Matilda in Los Angeles when the couple were telephoned with news of their nominations on 31 January 2006. An exhausted Ledger was mostly upset at having his sleep disturbed. Once he was fully awake, however, the importance of the nomination sank in – even if he remained unconvinced by the Academy Awards. 'I think it's a great honour to be in a movie that's been well received,' he acknowledged. 'Michelle and I definitely don't really sit around worrying about it. It's also a little surreal; kind of a strange concept to me that one performance or one movie can be compared or compete against another . . . It's an award season of opinions, so it's full of a false sense of success and failure.'

At the 78th Academy Awards ceremony, in March 2006, Philip Seymour Hoffman once again beat Ledger for the Best Actor award. Of its eight nominations, *Brokeback Mountain* only won three: Best Director for Ang Lee, Best Original Score for Gustavo Santaolalla and Best Adapted Screenplay for Larry McMurtry and Diana Ossana. The Best Picture award that many had assumed would go to *Brokeback Mountain* went instead to LA-set race drama *Crash*. If he was at all disappointed by not taking a deserved Best Actor award, Ledger kept his frustration to himself. At least one member of the *Brokeback* entourage, however, publicly denounced the Academy voters for having failed to award statuettes to Heath or his co-stars. Writing in the *Guardian* a few days after the Oscars ceremony, author Annie Proulx pulled no punches in delivering what she openly acknowledged to be a 'Sour Grapes Rant'. Of Philip Seymour Hoffman's victory for portraying true-life figure Truman Capote, she asked: 'But which takes more skill, acting a person who strolled the boulevard a few decades ago and who left behind tapes, film, photographs, voice recordings and friends with strong memories, or the construction of characters from imagination and a few cold words on the page?' She went on to refer to Best Picture winner *Crash* as 'Trash', and make several less-than-flattering comments about the internal prejudices she believed had influenced the Academy's final decision.

Whatever its wins or losses, the film had received help in securing its nominations from some superb reviews, some of which were the best of Ledger's career. *Variety* focused on 'an outstanding performance from Heath Ledger. Ledger is powerfully

impressive as a frightened, limited man ill-equipped to deal with what life throws at him. Mumbling, looking down, internalising everything, Ledger's Ennis at times looks as though he's going to explode from his inchoate feelings. [His] performance could scarcely be more different from his terrific work in the otherwise negligible *Lords of Dogtown*, and the combination makes it a dazzling year for Ledger.'

Kenneth Turan, in the *Los Angeles Times*, highlighted 'a powerful performance by a breathtaking Heath Ledger. Aside from his small but strong part in *Monster's Ball*, nothing in the Australian-born Ledger's previous credits prepares us for the power and authenticity of his work here as a laconic, interior man of the West, a performance so persuasive that *Brokeback Mountain* could not have succeeded without it. Ennis's pain, his rage, his sense of longing and loss are real for the actor, and that makes them unforgettable for everyone else.'

Peter Travers, writing in *Rolling Stone*, called *Brokeback Mountain* 'a landmark film and a triumph for Heath Ledger. Ledger's magnificent performance is an acting miracle. He seems to tear it from his insides. Ledger doesn't just know how Ennis moves, speaks and listens; he knows how he breathes. To see him inhale the scent of a shirt hanging in Jack's closet is to take measure of the pain of love lost.'

'After *Brokeback* I feel like I can take on anything. What could be more challenging or scary? Nothing scares me now.' – Heath Ledger

In the *San Francisco Chronicle*, film critic Mick La Salle wrote, 'Ledger makes the strongest choices. He gives Ennis a voice and mannerisms that are utterly idiosyncratic, and then inhabits those choices psychologically, making sense of the locked-down speech, the haunted look and the strong but diffident manner. He completely transforms himself. It's a performance that was thought through in detail and then lived in the moment, and it's one of the most beautiful things in movies this year.' Concluding the accolades, J. Hoberman wrote in *The Village Voice*, 'The movie earns its pathos through Ledger's performance.'

Inevitably, the film had also provoked controversy. One Salt Lake City cinema banned it outright, due to the gay sex scenes. Mike Thompson, executive director of the state's leading gay rights advocacy group, Equality Utah, said, 'It's just a shame that such a beautiful and award-winning film, with so much buzz about it, is not being made available to a broad Utah audience because of personal bias.'

For his part, Ledger was more amused than outraged. 'Personally, I don't think the movie is [controversial], but I think maybe the Mormons in Utah do . . . All of the American states, besides the odd one here and there, have ended up seeing it. It seems to have proven everyone wrong. I think people just want to see it so they can have an opinion on it. It's really interesting. I think it's going to turn into some kind of phenomenon.'

And a phenomenon is certainly what it became, marking a high point in terms of Heath Ledger's performance, the critical reaction and the audience response. 'After *Brokeback* I feel like I can take on anything,' he said. 'What could be more challenging or scary? Nothing scares me now.'

Heath and Michelle at the 78th Annual Academy Awards in Los Angeles, March 2006. The Oscars ceremony was the culmination of a six-month awards season that had taken the couple around the globe.

6. DARK STAR

'Music is such a pure expression of a song from the soul. It's always been a key that unlocked or enabled me to express anger or pains of any sort. It's always been a wonderful door opener for me in terms of being able to express, creatively and personally.'
– Heath Ledger

Maverick director Todd Haynes's offbeat biopic *I'm Not There* offered six actors the chance to play aspects of a Bob Dylan-esque character. Signing up for the film alongside Heath Ledger were *Batman Begins* star Christian Bale, young actor Marcus Carl Franklin, the iconic Richard Gere, up-and-coming Brit Ben Whishaw, and one actress, Cate Blanchett.

'In preparing *I'm Not There* I spent as much time studying Dylan's creative history as his literal one: his writing, his interviews, his films, as well as the music, writing, films and history that inspired him,' said Haynes of his unique approach to the offbeat film. 'The more I read the more I discovered how change – radical personal, artistic change – had defined his life. The only way to convey that would be to dramatise it, to literally distil his life and work into a series of separate selves and stories. The six characters that ultimately emerged seemed to encompass the dominant themes and instincts that informed his life and canon of work.'

Casting those six roles was an intuitive process for the director. 'I couldn't be more astounded by my actors in this film,' said Haynes. 'I provided all my lead actors with extensive visual material of Dylan and the stylistic references I was drawing on for each of their stories. In addition I made collections of songs and interviews from Dylan's career that inspired their roles. No one was asked to imitate him directly, but rather to make use of his cadences, looks and styles, as they pertained to their specific time in his life. The result is a range of interpretations of Dylan from the inside out.'

Heath joined the *I'm Not There* team in Montreal towards the end of the film's piecemeal July to September 2006 shooting schedule. He was following his partner Michelle Williams, who had been signed up to the film first to play Coco, the Edie

After an eighteen-month break from acting, Heath admitted that he was nervous about getting back in front of the camera.

Sedgwick-like lover of Blanchett's Jude. 'I said to my agent, "Is there something I can do on it? I'm going to be there anyway, looking after Matilda,"' admitted Heath.

His gambit worked when another actor dropped out, and director Todd Haynes soon had Ledger signed up to play one of the six aspects of Dylan portrayed in the film.

Despite playing a brief role, Heath approached the part with his usual fearless commitment. He was attracted to working on the film due to Haynes's 'wildly ambitious and incredibly creative' approach to filmmaking. 'I've always been picky in my choices,' said Ledger. 'But nowadays, I'm a lot more so. I was relieved of the duty of physically portraying Bob Dylan. I didn't really have to. No one's playing Bob Dylan. Even the title, *I'm Not There* . . . well, he's not there. They are sort of Dylan-inspired characters, but Cate Blanchett looks the most like Bob Dylan. It's very surrealistic and incredibly ambitious. I'm more curious about this than anything else I've been a part of.'

Music had always been an important part of Heath's off-screen life, but this was his first chance to play a musical icon on-screen. 'Music, on so many levels, has affected my life and still continues to,' said Heath. 'Music is such a pure expression of a song from the soul. It's always been a key that unlocked or enabled me to express anger or pains of any sort. It's always been a wonderful door opener for me in terms of being able to express, creatively and personally.'

'I usually go into a movie thinking that I'm hopeless, and I don't know how to do it any more, and I've forgotten it. This time I hadn't worked in a year-and-a-half, so it was worse.' – Heath Ledger on *I'm Not There*

Dylan's music allowed Heath to find a way into portraying the aspect of the character that Haynes had allocated him: Dylan as a happy family man, making films – a state that resonated with Heath's real life at the time. 'I found the connection in his lyrics, through his music, and through his poetry,' said Heath of his research for the role. 'It was an incredible experience. I consider Todd Haynes to be a genius. Cate Blanchett has such an incredible transformation in this movie. She walks, talks, sings and smells like Bob Dylan.'

Heath's character was called Robbie, representing Dylan's time as an actor and celebrity, and as a father trying to stay connected to his wife, played by Charlotte Gainsbourg. It was a role that Heath could empathise with. 'I can certainly relate to that, struggling to keep a consistency with family life, your social life and your professional life. It's both an annoyance and an addiction. I can definitely relate to it.'

Following *Lords of Dogtown*, this was the second time Ledger had attempted to portray a still-living real-life person on film, albeit a fantasy aspect of Dylan rather than a realistic portrait. That didn't stop Ledger from indulging in his usual research and preparation, despite the cameo nature of the role. 'I read the books, I watched the documentaries, my catalogue of Dylan's music was expanded,' said Heath of his process. 'I think it's all just to feed our superstitious needs to comfort ourselves [as actors]. You usually just have an innate understanding of what you need to do. Dylan was someone I felt I had to become obsessed with.'

Heath as one of six incarnations of Bob Dylan in Todd Haynes's cerebral rock biopic I'm Not There *(2007).*

Working on *I'm Not There* was the first time that Heath had come into contact with Christian Bale, soon to co-star with him in the hugely anticipated *Batman Begins* sequel *The Dark Knight*. 'I'm actually playing an actor who plays in a movie as a character, and his character is a Bob Dylanesque kind of guy played by Christian Bale. So I'm kind of playing Christian Bale.'

Shooting in Montreal, most of Heath's work was opposite Charlotte Gainsbourg, who played Claire, a French painter (and a film version of Sara Lownds, Dylan's first wife from 1965 to 1977). 'It's comforting knowing how detached we are [from a literal biography], and free because of that,' Ledger told *Premiere Magazine*. 'In conventional biopics, no matter how hard you try or how good the performances are, you're always defaming that person. You're always taking a little bit away from them. I think this film is attempting to honour Dylan in some way, as opposed to capture him.'

'In conventional biopics, no matter how hard you try or how good the performances are, you're always defaming that person. You're always taking a little bit away from them. I think this film is attempting to honour Dylan in some way, as opposed to capture him.'
– Heath Ledger

Left: Heath and director Todd Haynes share a joke between takes on the I'm Not There set in Montreal.
Above: Heath plays it cool as misogynistic husband and father Robbie Clark.

Robbie (Heath) and wife Claire (Charlotte Gainsbourg) discover that love is a burning thing.

Ledger's growing fame even played a part in securing the opportunity for the film unit to shoot in Montreal's Musee des Beaux Arts (which doubled for New York's Metropolitan Museum of Art for some scenes, and Paris' Louvre for others). 'This was the hardest location to secure,' said Haynes. 'We had to pull every string, use every connection. We finally got the okay after Heath posed for a photo with the museum director!'

Ledger's return to acting after an eighteen-month break spent with Matilda and Michelle meant that the actor was more troubled than usual when he reported to set. 'I was nervous [about this film] for many reasons,' Heath acknowledged, confirming that, after all this time, and the acclaim his most recent performances had received, he'd not lost his innate doubts about his own abilities. 'I usually go into a movie thinking that I'm hopeless, and I don't know how to do it any more, and I've forgotten it. This time I hadn't worked in a year and a half, so it was worse. Todd's such a wonderful man, and I was only working twelve days, so I was put to ease pretty quickly.'

To ensure their focus, each Dylan actor received their section of the script, complete with a mix-CD featuring the relevant Dylan songs. As a result, Ledger 'went back and discovered a whole bunch of his music that I'd never heard'. He then began work on capturing Robbie's voice. 'As an Australian, I always have to do an accent, so it's the first thing I start with. Once I have the voice, that's the line, and at the end of the line is a hook, and attached to that is the soul. Then the wardrobe and the fake beards are the icing on the cake.'

The finished movie rose to Heath's expectations and satisfied his idea that each of the Bob Dylan figures would remain enigmatic to the audience. 'I don't think you need to be a Dylan genius in order to appreciate it. It is a movie, there's no Q&A afterwards. The beauty of Todd's film is I can't tell you that I know anything more about Bob Dylan than you do. I think it's one of those films that you have to accept and invite [in] instead of trying to challenge and solve. Bob Dylan himself defies description, and I think Todd was aiming to represent him. He was not trying to sum him up or define him.'

For his part, Haynes was impressed with Heath's commitment and abilities. 'Heath has a little bit of James Dean in him, even physically, a kind of precocious seriousness,' Haynes claimed. 'Adult actors seem more and more infantile and refusing to grow up, middle-aged guys with their baseball caps, Heath is one of those young people who have a real intuition, a maturity beyond their years.'

Ledger was equally impressed with his *I'm Not There* director. 'Todd is an exciting filmmaker. Everyone I've spoken with so far has said that he's a genius and it's the most creative process they've all been a part of.'

Ledger was absent from the early October US premiere of the movie, allowing Michelle Williams to have the red carpet to herself and fuelling rumours that the pair's relationship was in trouble. *I'm Not There* opened in the US on just 130 screens in November 2007, taking just under $731,000 over the opening weekend. By the end of the film's theatrical run in March 2008, the film had grossed just over $4 million, with attendance no doubt boosted by interest in Ledger's performance following his death in January. In February, the film doubled the number of screens it was playing on, thanks to audience demand.

Most critics focused on Cate Blanchett's scene-stealing turn in *I'm Not There* (which earned her a Best Supporting Actress Oscar nomination), with most of the other actors contributing to the whole, but rarely being singled out for comment. Roger Ebert, in the *Chicago Sun-Times*, wrote of the film, '[It's] an attempt to consider the contradictions of Bob Dylan by building itself upon contradictions. [The] third [Dylan] is Heath Ledger, appearing in a Hollywood film, who settles down, gets married and has kids.' *Variety*'s Todd McCarthy noted, 'Ledger's Robbie is a moody actor who stars as a Dylan-like figure in a Hollywood film called *Grain of Sand*.' *Rolling Stone*'s Peter Travers wrote that Ledger 'digs deep into the challenging role of Robbie, an actor who plays Dylan in a movie'. Mick La Salle, writing in the *San Francisco Chronicle* noted Ledger played 'the celebrity Dylan, the one who must deal with the temptations and pressures of fame'. D. K. Holm in the *Vancouver Voice* wrote, 'Ledger plays Dylan as if he had become a philandering, married movie star (unlikely, given his looks and voice, as we now well know).' Peter Bradshaw, in the *Guardian*, saw Ledger as depicting 'Dylan's dark side: selfish, reactionary, misogynist', while Philip French in the *Observer* wrote that 'Robbie [is] an artist responding to the [Vietnam] war, a devoted,

frequently absent father of two daughters and unreliable husband to their mother.' It was a description that could soon be applied to Ledger's own domestic situation.

The paparazzi intrusion that had driven Heath and Michelle out of Australia and continued to haunt the relative sanctuary of their Brooklyn home proved increasingly difficult to evade, and the pair were shocked when in the summer of 2006 they discovered that photographers had even followed them on holiday to Mexico. 'Michelle was bathing topless,' recalled Heath, 'and she's very sensitive and private about her body in general. There was this fishing boat right off in the ocean just sitting there. . . and I'm like, "What are they catching right there?" And there was a guy with a paparazzi camera sitting in the back of the boat.' The bearded Ledger couldn't resist making rude hand gestures and held up a crude, hand-written sign (which read 'Fuck off') at the photographers, who – failing to miss an opportunity – happily snapped away and sold the resulting pictures.

'I can certainly relate to that, struggling to keep a consistency with family life, your social life and your professional life. It's both an annoyance and an addiction. I can definitely relate to it.' – Heath Ledger

Ironically, Heath felt that back in the US, he was of far less interest to the showbiz paparazzi packs. 'Some [Australian] paparazzi chant at me "Can't you take it Heath? You shouldn't be in showbiz if you can't take being followed and photographed. You need us, Heath." No I freakin' don't! The thing is I can't find anything that interesting about my life. Why follow me around with a camera? They have much bigger fish to fry than me over here [in the US].'

This was not the kind of fame the actor wanted. He was looking to be challenged in his on-screen roles, but off-screen he was not psychologically prepared to play the part of the big movie star, largely because he simply didn't see himself that way. While he had Michelle and Matilda to look after, he was able to deal with the anxiety caused by the unwanted attentions of the paparazzi. When he was without them and on his own, the attention of the press would become one among many sources of trouble for the sensitive young star.

In planning *I'm Not There*, Haynes had compiled a 'mood book' full of images, ideas and quotes that related to the film. For Robbie, Heath Ledger's Dylan, whose onscreen marriage fails, Haynes had written: 'A relationship doomed . . .'

Of course, Haynes could not have known that Heath and Michelle's relationship would be on the rocks by the time they'd both wrapped on *I'm Not There*. After shooting the film, in November 2006 the pair seemed to be discussing the possibility of getting married. Press reports even had them collecting a marriage licence in Brooklyn and planning a January wedding. The reports were denied and Ledger responded to the press interest: 'We try not to talk about it,' he said of a possible marriage, 'to keep it our own kind of thing. It's obviously very sacred. People write stories regardless. The stories haven't necessarily been bad, so we're letting people run

Heath and Michelle take daughter Matilda for a sunlit stroll.

with their assumptions.' Asked what would constitute a formal announcement of their wedding, Heath wittily replied, 'Photos of us wearing our wedding rings.'

Despite the public bravado, it seemed all was not well behind the scenes. Allegations were made after Heath's death that his hard-partying and escalating drug-taking caused him to drift apart from Michelle. However, the core problem was the same as one of the major issues that had split Ledger from Naomi Watts. As two much in-demand actors, with a very young daughter, Heath and Michelle found it difficult to balance their work (and the associated need to travel and be away from home for long periods of time) with their domestic lives.

According to Williams, talking to *Interview* magazine after Heath's death, the early days of their relationship were idyllic. 'The first six weeks of our daughter Matilda's life was this incredibly insular, protected time. It was just he and I and her, living in our new house in Brooklyn. No nanny, no help – not really even any family. A couple of friends came through, but we were really committed to forming a bond just between the three of us. Those six weeks were just blissful.'

It was a situation that couldn't last. Although the pair had managed to turn *I'm Not There* into a joint project, it was never going to be possible to do that with every film. From March to May 2007, Williams was committed to shooting thriller *Incendiary* with Ewan McGregor in the UK, while Ledger was due to begin work on *The Dark Knight* in March or April 2007, a seven-month commitment. It meant the pair would be apart for a long time. As Williams commented, 'That [domestic] bubble got broken with work.'

'When you're in a relationship with somebody who is also a public personality then it doubles the attention from the media.' – Michelle Williams

In March 2007, Michelle was in New York attending Fashion Week, while Heath was spotted carousing at Los Angeles nightclub Teddy's, 'surrounded by women' in the words of one report. According to a source quoted in the *New York Daily News*, the pair had 'a huge fight, and they're not speaking'. Quizzed by a reporter at Fashion Week about the status of her relationship with Ledger, Williams was said to have 'snapped'. Prior to that, Heath and Michelle had been seen together at the Independent Spirit Awards and at the Oscars, although it is possible they were keeping up something of a front for public consumption at a time they knew they were likely to be going their separate ways. 'When you're in a relationship with somebody who is also a public personality then it doubles the attention from the media,' said Michelle.

In August 2007, *Us Weekly* confirmed that Ledger and Williams had ended their relationship because of their busy work schedules. Neither Ledger nor Williams confirmed the rumour at that time, but by September 2007 Michelle's father, Larry, had informed the *Sydney Daily Telegraph* that the stars had indeed split up. Reporting their formal separation in September 2007, *Us Weekly* featured the usual 'anonymous source' who stated that the pair had gone their separate ways and had 'quietly and amicably split a few weeks ago. The relationship had been

Heath and Michelle walk hand in hand through the streets of Sydney.

rocky recently. They tried very hard to make it work, but finally decided to separate. They just grew apart. They have a beautiful daughter and they are both committed to being great parents.'

Following the split, Williams appeared keen to establish herself as the innocent party. 'Obviously so much has changed for me in the last few months that I don't really have an idea of what my life is going to be,' she told UK magazine *Wonderland*. 'I thought I knew certain things and it turned out that I didn't, so I don't really try and anticipate so much anymore. I'm not making any bets on the future.'

She found that her daughter, Matilda, was an important part of her ability to deal with the split from Heath. 'Going through a break-up is a really humanising experience. It just strips you to your core. You're nothing but feeling, nothing but emotion,' she said in an interview with *Vogue*. 'There's no difference between my break-up and anyone else's. I really only look back on [the relationship] with love because of my daughter. I can't regret a single second of it because of this little hell-raising cherub sleeping in the room next to me. She's bigger than any heartache could ever be.' The relationship had lasted for three years and Matilda was two-years-old at the time of the separation.

Williams's father, the then 65-year-old Larry Richard Williams (described by the media as 'an American futures trading guru and promotional speaker'), agreed that the reason for the separation was the intense pressure that the Hollywood system put on the couple. Williams, who had been released from prison on bail in May 2006 after being arrested in Australia on US tax evasion charges totalling $1.5 million between 1999 and 2001, told the Australian *Daily Telegraph*, 'We've known about their troubles for a while but it's always a very difficult thing in life when these things happen. I know Heath and Michelle still care about each other deeply and are very committed to being great parents to their daughter. You can never be stunned by what happens in Hollywood. I learned that when we were dealing with Michelle's career when she was younger. Michelle was grown up at sixteen, and just like Heath, her life has had an extremely fast pace to it. But they are both very talented artists and they live with their hearts. I feel tremendously for her, and for him and hope they will find what they want in life.'

Heath remained tight-lipped about events between him and Michelle, and quietly moved into a $23,000-a-month bachelor pad at 421 Broome Street in SoHo, NY. According to the *New York Post*, Heath was intent on having a bedroom in his new apartment decorated so that it looked exactly the same as Matilda's nursery at the family's previous home in Brooklyn, where Michelle still lived. A source told the newspaper, 'They are having them designed exactly the same so when she wakes up in Heath's place she won't feel displaced.'

'Heath really did take this break-up hard,' *People* Senior Editor J. D. Heyman told *Access Hollywood*. 'He loved the life that he had in Brooklyn, he loved being with Matilda. Particularly, whenever he was with Matilda people were blown away by his devotion to her.'

Heath's separation from Michelle and Matilda would have dire consequences for his state of mind and lifestyle over the following months.

Amidst rumours that their relationship was on the rocks, Heath and Michelle attended the 22nd Annual Film Independent Spirit Awards together in February 2007.

As he was shooting *I'm Not There*, Heath Ledger's name was linked to the role of the Joker in director Christopher Nolan's *Batman Begins* sequel, *The Dark Knight*. Among those also rumoured to be up for the showy role opposite Christian Bale as Batman were Robin Williams, Ledger's *A Knight's Tale* co-star Paul Bettany, and even the ever-so-serious Sean Penn. Any actor taking on the comic-book role would face a formidable challenge in following Jack Nicholson's acclaimed 1989 version of the character in director Tim Burton's first *Batman* movie.

The reasoning behind offering Ledger the part came from Nolan, who wanted a Joker who'd match Bale's brooding Batman, so he needed an actor of a similar age to the 32-year-old lead. Ledger was aware that he was no longer approached for leading parts in big action movies as he had turned down such roles too often, among them the 2004 remake of 1970s disaster movie *The Poseidon Adventure* and a major part in Baz Luhrmann's historical drama *Australia*. That didn't mean he wasn't interested in featuring in such films, it was just that the right combination of script, part and director had not come along yet. 'I would have fun making them, I just wouldn't want anyone to see them,' said Ledger of such blockbusters. 'If I could work out a deal where I could make the movies, run around, jump off things, shoot guns: OK, that would be fun. They're kind of mindless and you don't really have to try. You just say one line in each scene in your own way.'

> 'It's going to be more nuanced and dark and more along the lines of *A Clockwork Orange* feel. Which is, I think, what the comic book was after: less about his laugh and more about his eyes.' – Heath Ledger on playing the Joker

Given his recent track record for appearing in 'speciality' movies such as *Lords of Dogtown*, *Casanova*, *Candy* and *I'm Not There*, the thought of Heath putting on bizarre make-up and cavorting around Gotham City as the Joker came as a surprise to many of his fans. 'It's definitely going to stump people,' Heath said of his unexpected casting in *The Dark Knight*. 'I think [getting the role] was tougher for other people to comprehend than it was for me. It'll be more along the lines of how the Joker was meant to be in the comics, darker and more sinister.' Ledger was happy to admit that he was probably pretty low on most people's lists of potential Jokers for the movie. 'I wouldn't have thought of me, either, but it's obviously not going to be what Jack Nicholson did. It's going to be more nuanced and dark and more along the lines of *A Clockwork Orange* feel. Which is, I think, what the comic book was after: less about his laugh and more about his eyes.'

While he appreciated the 1989 Jack Nicholson version of the Joker, Heath saw that performance as something to react against, rather than emulate. 'I was definitely a fan of what Jack Nicholson did and the world Tim Burton created,' Ledger claimed. 'His performance was catering to that style of directing. It wasn't Chris Nolan. I can tell you now if Tim Burton directed *The Dark Knight* and he came and asked me to play the Joker, I'd say "No". I couldn't reproduce what Jack did. The reason why I confidently stepped into the [Joker's] shoes when Chris [Nolan] asked me [is because] I knew the world he created [in *Batman Begins*]. I

Michelle, Heath and Matilda out and about in Brooklyn. 'I just live a really normal life,' the actor said of his time there.

also knew there was a different angle to be taken. That's why I did it.'

Having been nothing if not candid about his much remarked-upon decision to turn down the lead role in *Spider-Man* during the early stages of his career, Heath continued to be surprisingly upfront about his disdain for films made from comic books. 'I actually hate comic-book movies, like fucking hate them,' he admitted. 'They bore me fuckless and they're just dumb. I thought what Chris Nolan did with *Batman Begins* was actually really good, really well directed, and Christian Bale was great in it. Not being a huge comic-book fan, and not one to really follow comic-book movies, I'm relaxed about it.'

There seemed to be little chance of Heath ever playing a comic-book superhero. 'With the tights and undies and the boots, I would just feel stupid and silly,' he confessed. 'I couldn't pull it off, and there are other people who can perfectly. I just couldn't take myself seriously. I feel like this is an opportunity to be in one and not [have to] do that. I just gravitated towards the villain role because I felt I had something to give to it. I instantly had an idea.'

Clearly, the attraction of *The Dark Knight* for Ledger was the possibility of playing a nuanced, complicated, yet truly evil character. 'He's going to be really sinister and it's going to be less about his laugh and his pranks and more about him just being a fucking sinister guy.'

Heath denied that his recent career travails and pressure from his agent had bounced him into seeking a role in a potential blockbuster. 'I'm sure they're super happy that I'm doing this,' he admitted, 'because this is the first time I've really taken something like that, so they're over the moon. But I think it's just going to be a really fun experience, and I love to dress up and wear a mask. I've seen a few interesting designs on the look and I think that it's going to look pretty cool.'

The screenplay and discussions with director Christopher Nolan convinced Ledger that he had something different to offer the role of the Joker. 'Somewhere inside of me, I knew instantly what to do with [this character],' said Ledger. 'I didn't have to search, I had a plan of attack. Part of me feels like I've been warming up to [playing the Joker] for years. In *The Brothers Grimm*, Terry Gilliam helped me put on a sort of clown act and adjust to that sort of pace. I feel it's something I know how to do. It'll be dark and sinister and exciting.'

'Somewhere inside of me, I knew instantly what to do with this character. I didn't have to search, I had a plan of attack. I feel it's something I know how to do. It'll be dark and sinister and exciting.' – Heath Ledger

Meeting with Nolan, Ledger was happy to discover that they were both on the same page when it came to the tone of the portrayal that would suit this new version of the character. 'When he explained to me the angle he wanted to take, I was like, "Yeah, I could do that,"' Ledger said. '[Nolan's] going to make it a lot more sinister, and we've got a little plan for him.'

Heath had to make a special trip in order to be able to read the then top secret screenplay, so paranoid were the movie's producers about 'spoilers' leaking on to the Internet. 'I went to [the screenwriter's] house in LA and he allowed me to read it. I had to read it at his house, he wouldn't let me take it home.'

Part of Heath's preparation for the role was the compilation of an 'inspiration book' he called the *Joker's Diary*. He started pulling material together for it four months before shooting started, and filled it with images and thoughts that he felt might help flesh out the Joker's story. The diary was more about mood and nuance of character than any hard, specific facts. The intention was to help him focus on an approach to the role. To that end, the diary included a list of terrible things the Joker might find funny, including AIDS. This suggested that Heath was planning a very dark take on the character. 'I sat around in a hotel room for about a month, locked myself away, formed a little diary and experimented with voices – it was important to try to find an iconic voice and laugh. I ended up landing more in the realm of the psychopath – someone with very little to no conscience towards his acts. I definitely have something up my sleeve,' hinted Heath. 'I want to be very sinister.'

Alone again. Neither Heath nor Michelle was willing to reveal the reasons for their separation, which became public knowledge in September 2007.

'The Joker cuts through the film. He's got no story arc, he's just a force of nature tearing through. Heath has given an amazing performance in the role, it's really extraordinary.' – Christopher Nolan

Although not a fan of the comic-book movies, Ledger was persuaded by Nolan to take a look at one particular acclaimed graphic novel, and the influence it had on Heath's portrayal was evident in the early trailers released to promote the film. 'The Killing Joke was the one that was handed to me. I think it's going to be the beginning of the Joker. I guess that book explains a little bit of where he's from, but not too much. From what I've gathered, there isn't a lot of information about the Joker and it's left that way.'

Director Nolan had been looking to work with Heath Ledger for some time, but none of the prospective projects had come to fruition. 'I met with Heath a couple of times over the years, but nothing really panned out until The Dark Knight,' Nolan told Entertainment Weekly. 'The first time I met him, I remember him explaining to me that he wanted to take his time as a young actor. He didn't want to be thrust centre stage before he achieved what he wanted to achieve. To be perfectly honest, that's a line I've heard from a lot of young actors. But he's the only one that I then paid $10 to go see do something really extraordinary – which was *Brokeback Mountain*. That was an incredible performance – such lack of vanity, such immersion. As an actor, Heath is fearless.'

Fearlessness was to be a watchword for Ledger's performance when he arrived on the Chicago location for *The Dark Knight* in March 2007. He'd prepared himself to go all out in his creation of this character, without worrying about where it may lead (or, indeed, what problems it might cause his future career). 'I feel like it's a character I've never done before,' Heath said of his version of the Joker. 'I'm not really thinking about the commercial consequences. Maybe I should be? At this point, it's just an exciting next step.' Ledger's Joker was to be a monster with no redeeming features. 'He's just out of control,' he acknowledged. 'He has no empathy. He's a sociopath, psychotic, mass-murdering clown. And I'm just thoroughly, thoroughly enjoying it.'

Nolan promised that *The Dark Knight* was a 'dark and complex story, and the villains are dark and complex as well'. Cast alongside Bale and Ledger were Aaron Eckhart as Gotham City District Attorney Harvey Dent, who starts the movie as a handsome lawman but ends up as Two-Face, the villain driven insane by disfiguring wounds, and Cillian Murphy, who reprised his role from *Batman Begins* as the Scarecrow. The film shot in Chicago, Los Angeles and London between April and November 2007 under the codename *Rory's First Kiss*, following a month of pre-production in March.

Balancing several villains and one superhero proved not to be a problem for Nolan, who felt that Ledger's Joker was the centre of the movie. 'The Joker cuts through the film,' said Nolan. 'He's got no story arc, he's just a force of nature tearing through. Heath has given an amazing performance in the role, it's really extraordinary.'

Images of Ledger as the Joker emerged long before the film was due for release in July 2008. His gruesome, carelessly applied and smudged Joker make-up was an instant signal that he was taking a different approach to the role. 'I don't know if I was

fearless,' Ledger told *Empire* magazine. 'I definitely feared it, although anything that makes me afraid excites me at the same time. I certainly had to put on a brave face.'

Of his leading villain, Nolan said, 'Heath's not doing any particular thing, he's just inhabiting the character in very much the way I'd hoped from a psychological perspective. He's really created something that I think is going to be quite terrifying.'

Heath finally achieved in the Joker something he'd been trying to do for a while: inhabit the deep psychology of his character. He wasn't trying to play the role, he *became* the role. The nearest he'd come previously to perfecting this approach was with Ennis Del Mar in *Brokeback Mountain*. Now, he was applying the same technique of inhabiting the character's mental state, but was this time playing a psychopathic criminal. It was an unorthodox approach that was going to take its toll on the young actor. It seemed to be having the desired effect, though, with co-star Michael Caine reporting that Ledger's performance was so terrifying the veteran actor sometimes found himself forgetting his own lines. 'You've never seen anything like it,' said Caine. 'He is very, very scary.'

'That was one of the goals, yeah,' confirmed Ledger of the terrifying nature of his Joker. 'He has zero empathy. It's the most fun I've had with a character and probably will ever have. The movie itself is far exceeding my expectations. I think it's going to be a really fun movie to watch. There's a bit of everything in him: *A*

'He has no empathy. He's a sociopath, psychotic, mass-murdering clown. And I'm just thoroughly, thoroughly enjoying it.' – Heath Ledger

Clockwork Orange, Sid Vicious . . .'

During shooting, Nolan noted that Heath's '[interpretation of the Joker is] very much a character, an iconic character, and very much not [Heath]. So to watch it is actually enthralling and captivating and exciting – all those positive things.'

'Chris has given me free rein,' said Heath. 'There are no real boundaries to what the Joker would say or do. Nothing intimidates him, and everything is a big joke.'

Making the movie was no joke for Heath, though. 'It's definitely a machine and you really feel it when you're on set,' he said of big-budget filmmaking at the blockbuster franchise level. He also had comic-book-fan interest to deal with. 'The awareness of it is creepy. I could not turn down this character. It's sinister and psychotic and he's bloodthirsty. It's just twisted and I've really enjoyed it.' Even though the role meant once again hiding his natural Australian accent: 'The Joker,' acknowledged Heath, 'is definitely an American.'

Heath Ledger's life was on the verge of major change. The idyll of his relationship with Michelle Williams had come to a sad end with their separation. After his joy at becoming a father, Heath found himself fulfilling the role on a part-time basis. To escape his anguish at this turn of events, he threw himself into his work. The role of the Joker came along at just the right time, providing the disturbed actor with an all-consuming part in which he could get lost. The problem was, Ledger's reaction to the disturbing turn his life had taken meant he'd become lost forever.

In The Dark Knight *(2008) Heath made the disturbing and iconic role of the Joker very much his own.* '*You've never seen anything like it,' said co-star Michael Caine. 'He is very, very scary.*'

7. THE LAST DAYS

'I feel in a sense ready to die, because you
live on in your child. I feel good about dying now,
because I feel like I'm alive in her.'
– Heath Ledger

During the latter half of 2007, Heath Ledger was reeling from his separation from Michelle Williams and his two-year-old daughter, Matilda. It was an unhealthy state of affairs for a fragile actor who already suffered for his art. Having developed the technique of full immersion in his characters, particularly in *Brokeback Mountain* and *The Dark Knight*, Ledger found it difficult to shake them off when filming finished. His anxieties about his screen performances and what they might mean for his career fuelled his growing insomnia. Seeking relief, the otherwise healthy 28-year-old increasingly turned to prescription medicines to help him relax and sleep. His journeys around the world to shoot movies – at this time he was hopping between London and New York shooting on Terry Gilliam's *The Imaginarium of Doctor Parnassus* – meant that he'd often draw on the services of several doctors to address his sleeplessness and general anxiety. It appears that, for a long time, Heath Ledger was a tragic accident just waiting to happen.

According to *Us Weekly*, Michelle Williams had wanted Heath to enter drug rehab as far back as March 2006, pointing to a possible deeper, long-standing drug problem for the star. Describing Ledger as 'depression prone', the magazine claimed he had a 'cocaine, heroin and drink abuse' problem, and that Williams was desperate to help him beat his demons. 'Heath Ledger was a partier,' *People* Senior Editor J. D. Heyman claimed to *Access Hollywood*. 'He liked to go out, he was a known user of drugs, he used cocaine. He had a lifestyle that really wasn't – at least in Michelle Williams's eyes – compatible with raising a child and continuing in that relationship. Even though their relationship did not work out, she did love Heath – she loved him very much.'

*After his death, lurid media rumours about Heath Ledger's
alleged drug use and hedonistic lifestyle were rife.*

After Ledger's death, Hollywood personal assistant Rebecca White revealed new details of Ledger's alleged drug habits to the *Mail on Sunday*. 'I knew Heath used drugs because the first time I met him, at Puff Daddy's house in Los Angeles, Heath asked [model] Naomi [Campbell] for cocaine. At another party in Paris, Heath took at least six Ecstasy pills, popped them in his mouth all at once and swigged them with a bottle of champagne.'

White also claimed that the relationship between Heath and Michelle was doomed from the start. 'It was this movie-set romance and Michelle got unexpectedly pregnant. It absolutely would not have lasted if she hadn't [got pregnant]. He was still seeing other women. Heath was an Adonis and she was dowdy and not in his league – career-wise or looks-wise – and no one could understand why they got together.'

The end of the relationship, White alleged, stemmed from Ledger's increasing recklessness with drugs and changes in his lifestyle. 'He was a partygoer and Michelle was quite straight. But when she got pregnant, Michelle was determined to have the baby. Heath wanted to do the right thing and stick by her. Michelle kicked Heath out because he would be showing up all hours of the night with this band of hangers-on and doing drugs.'

Adding to Heath's problems – according to White – was the fear that after the break-up Michelle was seeking sole custody of their daughter, Matilda. 'Michelle started to talk about going for sole custody,' claimed White, seemingly the only source for this information. 'She wanted to be responsible 100 per cent. She felt Heath couldn't be responsible for the baby because he wasn't responsible for himself. He got deeper and deeper into drugs as his fears of losing Matilda increased.'

'It was an exhausting process. I actually had quite a bit of time off between scenes – weeks sometimes. But it was required, because whenever I was working it exhausted me to the bone. At the end of the day, I couldn't move. I couldn't talk. I was absolutely wrecked.' – Heath Ledger on playing the Joker

Ledger's lifestyle could easily have dramatically changed and taken a turn for the worse when he was newly on his own. 'Heath was a very shy, insecure man,' White persisted. 'In celebrity circles you need something to ground you, and for him that was being a father and the idea that Michelle might still take him back and they might still be a family. Even though he was seeing other women, there was one side of him that still wanted their relationship to work. But there was also the side that depended on drugs because he felt like a fish out of water.'

Rebecca White had previously sold stories about the drug excesses of various celebrities that she claimed to have witnessed during her time as PA to notoriously difficult supermodel Naomi Campbell. Whether her allegations concerning Heath's substance abuse were the words of a genuine Hollywood insider or merely a disgruntled one-time subordinate who knew that sensationalism pays well is unclear, although her apparent knowledge of the intimate inner workings of Heath and Michelle's relationship seems somewhat suspect, to say the least.

When Ledger and Williams split in September 2007, the official explanation was pressure of work, but could Heath's supposed escalating drug use have been a factor? In the past, Heath had convincingly claimed limited experience of drugs, suggesting he'd indulged in little beyond smoking pot. Moving out of the family home and living on his own, with only occasional access to his daughter, was a severe blow to Heath, who tended to be anxious and distressed at the best of times.

Ledger's anxiety over the separation from Michelle and Matilda built on lingering bad feelings from his performance as the Joker in *The Dark Knight*, which wrapped in November 2007, and the harassment he'd suffered from the paparazzi over several years. 'It was an exhausting process,' Ledger had claimed of immersing himself in the psycho role. 'I actually had quite a bit of time off between scenes – weeks sometimes. But it was required, because whenever I was working it exhausted me to the bone. At the end of the day, I couldn't move. I couldn't talk. I was absolutely wrecked. If I had to do that every day, I couldn't have done what I did. The schedule really permitted me to exhaust myself.'

'Last week I probably slept an average of two hours a night. I couldn't stop thinking. My body was exhausted, and my mind was still going.' – Heath Ledger

Overactive at the best of times, Heath found he had even more trouble sleeping while making *The Dark Knight* as he had added difficulty shaking off the complex performance he was giving. 'Last week I probably slept an average of two hours a night,' he claimed as production came to an end. 'I couldn't stop thinking. My body was exhausted, and my mind was still going.' One night he took a sleeping pill called Ambien to help him rest, but it failed to work. He found himself taking a second, only to fall into a disturbed stupor and wake up just an hour later, his mind still racing. 'It can be a little distressing to over-intellectualise yourself.'

Ledger's anxiety resulting from his performances was partly what had led to his critically acclaimed turn in *Brokeback Mountain*. So focused was he on becoming Ennis Del Mar, body and soul, he'd also had trouble leaving the character behind. 'I'd go back to my trailer every night torturing myself, feeling like a failure. But I'd wake up the next morning wanting to do better,' said Ledger of his work with Ang Lee.

This focus resulted in a career-making performance, but at great cost to the actor's own peace of mind. Heath lacked self-confidence when it came to his acting, despite the acclaim he'd enjoyed and appearances that might have suggested otherwise. He felt he hadn't earned the positive notices, as he lacked stage experience and had not been formally trained as an actor. Heath expressed his fear that he'd be 'found out' many times: 'Quite literally, after getting a role, I'll call my agent and say, "How do I get out of this? I can't do it, I shouldn't do it. I fooled them [last time]." I always think that I'm going to fail. It seems to be a necessary process of mine, to focus [on] and defeat my own anxieties.'

The Oscar nomination for *Brokeback Mountain* didn't help Heath to relax. 'I think there's a new level of interest, but I haven't really acted on it, since the only thing I've really done since is the Todd Haynes film and the Joker.'

'Heath has touched so many people on so many different levels during his short life but few had the pleasure of truly knowing him.'
– Kim Ledger

'He had a talent for everything that he put his mind to, pretty much, so he didn't know limits. Maybe he had never been told that he couldn't do something, so everything was possible for him.'
– Michelle Williams

Left: *Heath once again finds himself the object of unwanted attention while enjoying a coffee and cigarette.*
Above: *Heath embraces his most important role; that of father to young Matilda Rose.*

Making films was not easy for Heath Ledger, and the more he got caught up in his screen characters – perhaps in an effort to escape his real life, which seemed to be spiralling out of his control – the more difficulty he created for himself. 'As actors we're asked to bare our souls and it's just whether or not you're prepared to do that. What I get out of it is quite therapeutic: I get to scream. Acting is also a form of escapism. You put on costumes, but what you're escaping from most of the time is life, the social world. [Making] a film is excruciating. I lose sleep, I'm anxious, excited and nervous and the adrenaline's pumping. That's the only way that I can act.'

The combination of anxiety about his crumbling personal life, his professional prospects, harassment by the media and the need to build a career on the back of his Oscar nomination, as well as the ghosts of the most recent characters he'd played, may have been enough to drive Ledger to escape into the world of drugs. He then found himself increasingly relying on sleeping pills and prescription medicines to force his body and mind to relax. 'I need to do something with this head because sometimes I just don't sleep, it just keeps ticking,' he told *The Times*, admitting to his growing Ambien habit. Even with the pills, he could only manage two hours sleep a night. It was not a situation that could go on forever.

Heath Ledger's final year of life began with the revelation of a characteristic act of kindness. Heath's old acting buddy Martin Henderson featured in the press, telling the tale of how Heath had helped him out financially back in 2000 when his career took a dip. 'I was just broke. Heath was very supportive and generous, giving me some money that he got on the movie [*The Patriot*],' said Henderson.

'Quite literally, after getting a role, I'll call my agent and say, "How do I get out of this? I can't do it, I shouldn't do it." I always think that I'm going to fail. It seems to be a necessary process of mine, to focus on and defeat my own anxieties.' – Heath Ledger

While denying rumours of a 'secret wedding' to Michelle Williams, Ledger found himself featured in *New Woman*'s January 2007 issue, coming at Number 22 in the Top 100 'Hottest Men on the Planet' list. Although he beat the likes of Joaquin Phoenix and Leonardo DiCaprio, Heath came way behind the top of the list which featured Brad Pitt, his *Brokeback Mountain* co-star Jake Gyllenhaal and *Ned Kelly*'s Orlando Bloom as the top three. *Brokeback Mountain* and Ledger were back in the news in February, when the film won the 'best screen kiss' award from DVD-rental firm LOVEFiLM.com, beating *Gone With the Wind* and *Dirty Dancing* in the sexy smooching stakes.

More importantly, in February 2007 Heath teamed up with his friend singer/songwriter Ben Harper to start new music label called Masses Music Co. 'Heath's really into music and he knows what he's talking about, he's my manager but he's more like my big brother,' said Masses' first signing, 17-year-old Australian Grace Woodroofe. Ledger unveiled the label's first act at the 9 February opening of Los Angeles lounge Edison, after signing her up personally when he 'fell in love with' her voice. Heath directed Woodroofe's music video for a cover version of David

Bowie's 'Quicksand'. Sara Cline, a partner in Masses with Ledger and Matt Amato, told *Interview* magazine, 'Heath had come into the Masses and one of the first things he said was, "You know, there's this girl, Grace Woodroofe, this Australian artist. She's seventeen-years-old and she's got this incredible voice and I want to produce her album." And we all kind of looked at each other and said, "Well, none of us have any experience with that." But he said, "No, we'll figure it out. We'll just fly her out to Los Angeles and we'll get it done." And, of course, before you knew it, we had this girl literally on our doorstep with her guitar. So we did some recordings that turned out really beautifully, and Heath directed a music video for her.'

'I really try not to be concerned about the reaction out there to what I do. Otherwise it would taper my choices. So it really doesn't bother me.' – Heath Ledger

'I do have some wonderful distractions,' Heath said of his life off-camera in 2007. 'I have a music label and I direct music videos and so I immerse myself in a different industry which kind of keeps acting really fresh for me.' Ledger directed several music videos, including Ben Harper's 'Morning Yearning' and videos for 'Cause an Effect' and 'Seduction Is Evil (She's Hot)' for Australian hip-hop artist N'fa. During one of his video shoots, Ledger was buying his LA property from Ellen DeGeneres, and the pair had become friends. 'He and Michelle came over to the house once,' remembered DeGeneres, 'and they were really late because he was directing a Ben Harper video. He was coming straight from that and he was telling us about it and how much he loved it. And then we played poker and he proceeded to take all of our money.'

Also planned was a video for Modest Mouse. Front-man Isaac Brock revealed, 'Heath wanted to do a video for one of the songs that didn't make it on the record [album *We Were Dead*], "King Rat". Terry Gilliam was going to help animate it. Heath and I had a mutual friend and, when we were in Australia, my fiancé and some of us in the band went out on a boat with him and his family and friends and talked about the idea.' This was one of several music-related projects that Heath had lined up which didn't come to pass.

By June 2007, Heath was deeply immersed in Joker duties for *The Dark Knight* in Chicago, with the project funnelling $45 million into the city's economy through the hiring of 390 locals, 250 'day players' and some 6,000 extras. On Monday, 25 June, Heath attended the premiere of *Rescue Dawn*, supporting the movie's leading man and his *The Dark Knight* co-star Christian Bale.

During filming on the Batman movie in August, Heath bravely rushed to co-star Maggie Gyllenhaal's rescue when her skirt caught fire on the set. Jake's sister was filling Katie Holmes's role of Rachel Dawes from the first film in the sequel when a special-effects generator toppled over and sent flames shooting up her skirt. No one was injured, and Ledger emerged as the hero of the moment.

Later in August, Heath was on publicity duties to support the opening of *I'm Not There* and then attended the wrap party at Carnivale, a Chicago nightclub, to mark the end of principal photography on *The Dark Knight* on 29 August, no doubt with some great relief as he could now hope to begin to put the Joker behind him. He spent much of the party playing poker, a favourite game of his.

In September came the confirmation of Heath's split from Michelle Williams, and the troubled actor adopted a low-key lifestyle after moving into his new Broome Street apartment. He was working on press and promotion for *I'm Not There*, but reporters were warned not to ask Ledger about his private life. Amid speculation that Ledger might return to Australia, an anonymous family member (understood to be Ledger's father, Kim) was quoted in the press as saying, 'His future's in Hollywood. He doesn't really have a reason to come back.' That same month, Ledger was absent from the New York premiere of *I'm Not There*, even though (or perhaps because) Michelle Williams was in attendance.

One of the reasons for Heath signing on to Todd Haynes's Bob Dylan biopic *I'm Not There* became clearer at September 2007 Venice Film Festival press conference. Heath was planning to make a biopic himself, about tragic English folk singer/songwriter Nick Drake. 'I was obsessed with his story and his music and I pursued it for a while,' said Ledger of the 'mysterious' performer who overdosed on prescription anti-depression medication in 1974 at the age of 26. While taking time away from acting to look after Matilda, Heath had also been working on a screenplay for his planned Drake feature. 'It kind of died away, faded away,' he said of the project. 'He was a very mysterious figure and I felt like I would be taking too many liberties. I still have hopes to kind of tell his story one day.'

'I think he was a bit damaged by the American publicity machine. He lost those crucial years between 19 and 24, when you discover who you are as an adult.'
– Neil Armfield

Director Todd Haynes was aware of Ledger's plans, and saw the would-be screenwriter's doubts about being able to do the topic justice. 'Trying to squeeze this complex, beautiful, and mysterious subject into the confines of the traditional biopic he found reprehensible and kind of cruel,' said Haynes to *New York* magazine. 'He was starting to approach it through a more allegorical method, where it was going to be about a woman travelling on a train ride through Europe – which Nick Drake I think did do – and he was going to have Michelle play that role.'

In pursuit of his obsession, Ledger shot and edited a music video for a Drake song called 'Black Eyed Dog', named after Winston Churchill's description of depression as a 'black dog'. It was also supposedly the last song Drake recorded before his untimely death. After Ledger's own death, many saw the video as prescient. It features a stark black-and-white composition, and the 'action' consisted mainly of the long-haired, unkempt director himself, who at the song's end is seen drowning himself in a bathtub. The short was filmed in November 2007 and was included in a multi-media instalment about Drake called *A Place to Be*. The project was only screened in public twice before the actor's death, and the Ledger family later said the 'Black Eyed Dog' video would not be publicly released. 'He did it in one day in London. He went out and shot it in black and white – it's the only video

An uneasy-looking Heath sat in the front row for a Marc Jacobs show during New York Fashion Week in September 2007, one of his first public appearances following his and Michelle's separation.

that he himself appears in. It is just a stunning piece of work,' said Haynes.

Following his death, fans would look at the clips of the Nick Drake video released to news programmes and wonder if it was a message from the troubled actor. 'Was it a clue, was it a message, or was it a cry out that he was going through a dark period in his life?' asked Australian newspaper columnist and Nick Drake fan Anita Quigley. 'You have the eerie link of Nick Drake dying of a prescription overdose – was it deliberate or not? – and then Heath Ledger dying of an overdose of prescription drugs. I wonder what that says about Heath's mood or personality. Was he in a dark time in his life when he shot [the video]?'

Ledger's own musical tastes were revealed when several of his favourite tracks were played at his funeral, including 'Past And Pending' by The Shins; 'The Times They Are A–Changin'' by Bob Dylan; 'Superstition' by Stevie Wonder; and 'Wish You Were Here' by Pink Floyd.

Michelle Williams had a simpler explanation for Heath's interest in music and directing videos than seemingly covert cries for help: 'Music became more important to him because he could do something creative without it costing him his privacy. He could be more in the background. He could be in charge, but invisible.'

'As actors we're asked to bare our souls and it's just whether or not you're prepared to do that. What I get out of it is quite therapeutic: I get to scream. Acting is also a form of escapism. You put on costumes, but what you're escaping from most of the time is life, the social world. Making a film is excruciating.' – Heath Ledger

The abandoned Nick Drake biopic project wasn't the only attempt Heath Ledger made to step behind the camera. Having been a junior chess champion in New South Wales at the age of ten, Heath had kept up his interest and played regularly at the Washington Square Park in Brooklyn. Ledger was hoping to direct a movie about chess based on Walter Tevis's novel *The Queen's Gambit*, about an orphan girl who becomes a chess prodigy, with the lead role offered to *Juno* star Ellen Page. Heath had been focused on the project for much of 2007, working with veteran screenwriter Allan Scott (who'd scripted *Don't Look Now* in 1973) on adapting the novel.

'The movie is about chess,' said Scott, 'and what is a little-known fact is that Heath was very close to being on the grandmaster level. He was a chess whiz, and he intended to get his grandmaster rating before he started shooting the picture.' Eerily, and in another seeming premonition of the actor's death, in the screenplay the principal character wrestles with addiction to prescription drugs – obtained from foreign doctors – and at one point she's to be seen lying on a bed surrounded by alcohol and pills. The screenplay describes the scene: 'Her suitcase lies open on the bed, clothes spilling everywhere. There are at least a dozen bottles of tranquilliser pills lying in the suitcase, stuffed into every corner, each with Mexican labels. She opens one of these – grabs a bottle of liquor – and drinks direct from the bottle to swallow two pills.'

Scott had optioned the book himself in 1990, opening out its internalised story. Among the directors attached at one time were Michael Apted and Bernardo Bertolucci. 'A year ago I had calls from three people who wanted to direct it,' claimed

Scott. 'And of the three, I found Heath was the one I wanted to work with. He was passionate about it; he was an intense, interested young man and I was drawn to him immediately. We spoke and spoke about the project over the phone, and then eventually got round to meeting up over it towards the end of last year. We spent a lot of time over the last three months working on his vision. I did draft after draft and he gave his input and we met several times in New York and here [London], where he was spending a lot of his time. We had got to the stage where we had sent the script to Ellen [Page]. Heath was full of ideas for the other cast, mainly from his list of acting friends. We were planning to make the movie at the end of 2008.'

Ledger's involvement in the project even extended to suggesting appropriate music to use, including Rosemary Clooney's 'This Ole House'. Scott found his email inbox filling up with messages from Heath containing his thoughts about the chess movie, often sent in the middle of the night.

Heath was planning on involving his Masses colleagues in the production of *The Queen's Gambit*, and Sarah Cline had read the book in preparation. 'Immediately this book sparked something within us and tapped into our sensibility; it is a great actor's piece, a formidable director's canvas, and a story that strongly champions the resilience of the human spirit. It's smart, powerful, and moving.'

Following Heath's death, screenwriter Allan Scott was hopeful that the Masses group would move the project forward and find a suitable replacement director. 'It's just a question of waiting for the right opportunity and getting the right director,' said Scott of the project that would have been Heath Ledger's directorial debut. 'I thought Heath was that. Although it's a very commercial subject, it will be seen as an art-house movie, so you need to bring in strong actors and make a beautiful film in order to have a hope of having a break-out success.'

'I do have some wonderful distractions. I have a music label and I direct music videos and so I immerse myself in a different industry which kind of keeps acting really fresh for me.' – Heath Ledger

During his last year, Ledger considered and rejected several starring film roles, including a part opposite Rachel Weisz in a romantic drama, *Dirt Music*. The movie was to be an adaptation of a Tim Winton novel about a couple in a loveless relationship, set in a remote fishing village on the West Australian coast. Australian director Phillip Noyce had optioned the novel and asked Heath to star. Ledger also went head to head with James Bond actor Daniel Craig to play the part of Satan in a $130 million feature film based on *Paradise Lost*, John Milton's 17th-century epic poem which tells the story of Lucifer's fall from grace and the temptation of Adam and Eve.

In October 2007, *A Place To Be – A Celebration of Nick Drake* took place at American Cinemateque in Los Angeles, billed as featuring 'the world premiere of short film homages to the singer titled *Their Place: Reflections On Nick Drake*, created by fans including actor Heath Ledger.' It was one of the very few public screenings of Heath's music video work.

That same month, Ledger began work on *The Imaginarium of Doctor Parnassus*, the film that was to reunite him with his *The Brothers Grimm* director, Terry Gilliam. It would also turn out to be his final screen performance. When he appeared on set in December 2007, Ledger was looking to learn from Gilliam as he thought about making his own movie. In an interview with *Variety*, Gilliam told the trade paper, 'Heath is extraordinary. He's just so good, and he's going to be a film director. He's watching everything, and he's going to be a much better director than I will ever be.'

The Imaginarium of Doctor Parnassus was an original script the director had co-written with Charles McKeown, telling the story of ancient magician Doctor Parnassus (Christopher Plummer) who makes a deal with the Devil (singer/actor Tom Waits), allowing audiences at his travelling show to take a trip through his magic mirror into a fantasy land. When an outsider – Toby (played by Ledger) – joins the troupe, he finds himself on a magical quest to save Parnassus's daughter (Lily Cole) who's been taken by the Devil.

'Music became more important to him because he could do something creative without it costing him his privacy. He could be more in the background. He could be in charge, but invisible.' – Michelle Williams

Model-turned-actress Cole related fond memories of the time she spent on-set with Ledger to Luke Davies in a piece written for Australian magazine *The Monthly*, claiming that Heath had taken her under his wing, offering reassurance when she was plagued by nerves, allowing her to stay at his London home when he was away, and giving her the password to his personal computer so that she could access his iTunes song collection. 'He wanted everyone to share what he loved,' Cole said. 'He was just like . . . give. *Give*. You know what I mean?'

During an optimistic phone call from the chilly London set, Heath would tell his agent, Steve Alexander: 'I'm really getting the hang of this at last. I think I'm beginning to know what I'm doing.'

'I'm trying to bring a bit of fantasticality to London,' said Terry Gilliam, who'd set the tale of his 1000-year-old magician in the present day as 'an antidote to modern lives. I loved this idea of an ancient travelling show offering the kind of storytelling and wonder that we used to get, to people who are just into shoot-'em-up action films. Parnassus is trying to bring amazement to people, and not doing a very good job of it, because they aren't paying attention to him. But if they will enter his mirror, and allow their imagination to mix with his, they enter these extraordinary worlds, and they come back transcendent – or they strangely disappear.' Gilliam knew the key to getting the $30 million he needed to make a movie like this was down to the casting. '[I have] to get Johnny Depp or Heath Ledger. If big-name actors didn't want to work with me for bad money, I wouldn't be able to do it.'

Ledger's death would present Gilliam with something of a dilemma when it came to potentially finishing his movie without its star name.

While he was reportedly desperate to get back together with Williams and his daughter,

Heath and Lily Cole on the London set of Terry Gilliam's The Imaginarium of Doctor Parnassus *(2009).*

Heath Ledger reverted to old romantic habits when he developed a friendship with 38-year-old Danish supermodel Helena Christensen, ten years his senior. Tabloid reports had them acting in an 'intimate' manner in a variety of New York locations, and Heath was seen to be hanging out with Helena while she conducted press interviews. Another habit Heath had was to date his movie co-stars, so it was little surprise when the New York newspapers also linked him with his *The Four Feathers* co-star Kate Hudson. During late 2007, he was also seen spending time with ex-girlfriend Heather Graham and with troubled young actress Lindsay Lohan and even attending a launch party for Naomi Watts's new movie *Eastern Promises*. Australian model/actress Gemma Ward (from Perth, like Heath) was also on the growing list of young (and not so young) women the press connected to Ledger. None of this was particularly surprising or shocking behaviour for a newly single 28-year-old film star.

'Heath is extraordinary. He's just so good, and he's going to be a film director. He's watching everything, and he's going to be a much better director than I will ever be.'
— Terry Gilliam

Towards the end of 2007, friends, relations and hangers-on seemed to encounter two very different versions of Heath Ledger. According to his family and Michelle Williams, Heath was a responsible family man devoted to his daughter, as well as being clean and sober. According to New York's show-business demi-monde, Ledger was instead a drug-abusing, womanising, party animal simply out for a good time, paying little regard to the consequences.

It is possible both of these seemingly conflicting versions of Heath Ledger contain within them some degree of truth. Ledger was overjoyed to be a father and his separation from Williams had hit him hard, reflected in his almost total silence on the subject. It's possible he'd had drink and drug issues, as alleged by those who claimed Williams had tried to force him into rehab. These problems may have escalated once he was on his own, forced into a bachelor lifestyle. He was a young movie star on his own in New York: wouldn't attending celebrity parties, with all that entails, come naturally? Ledger was never particularly good at being alone: on his own he could be overwhelmed by self-pity, depression and his anxiety about his career, his abilities and the paranoia that he was being stalked by aggressive paparazzi. No wonder he felt the need of distraction among company.

Christmas 2007 saw Heath return to Perth, with Gemma Ward, and spend the holidays with his family and her model sister Sophie. They were spotted at the movies and in restaurants, either as a couple or with members of Heath's family in tow. At that time, Michelle Williams was in Sweden, with Matilda, filming on *Mammoth*, a drama about an American businessman's relationship with his family's Filipino maid. Heath tried to keep a low profile while back in Perth, fearful that the local paparazzi would harass him if they knew he was there. Those who saw him during this period reckon he was on edge and couldn't relax, but they put this down to him fretting over the failure of his relationship with Williams and worries about his future access to his daughter. In an interview during his promotional work on *I'm Not There* (the last film he'd do promotional interviews for), Heath said, 'I feel in a sense ready to die, because you live on in your child. I feel good about dying now, because I feel like I'm alive in her.'

Before and after his Christmas 2007 trip home, Ledger had become a regular at trendy New York nightspot Beatrice Inn, located close to his vast five-room Broome Street bachelor pad. The Inn attracted New York's hip young Hollywood crowd, including names like Owen Wilson, Kate Moss, Kirsten Dunst and Mary-Kate Olsen (with whom Ledger was to be linked posthumously). A long feature article in *New York* magazine carried quotes from an unnamed young woman who claimed to have had a brief three-month fling with Heath during this period. Invited back to Broome Street, the woman claimed, 'We went over and hung out, played backgammon.' She claimed that Ledger was rather quiet, introverted but friendly, and certainly sober and not doing any kind of drugs. 'Heath was obviously in a vulnerable state,' she claimed. 'He didn't like being this star. He was kind of quiet unless he was comfortable, and it really seemed like he was just trying to have fun. He had a party at his loft once, and it was really crazy. There were drugs there, but he didn't touch them. I saw [drugs] offered to him multiple times. Ecstasy, cocaine, even prescription stuff – but he never touched it. I was with him at least a dozen times, and he was always sober. Just cigarettes.' This was yet another piece of the seemingly contradictory Heath Ledger jigsaw puzzle that made up the actor's final three months.

'I'm really getting the hang of this at last. I think I'm beginning to know what I'm doing.' – Heath Ledger

Early in January 2008, Heath had been in London for location shooting on Terry Gilliam's *The Imaginarium of Doctor Parnassus*. Spotted in and around the South Bank of the Thames, filming at Blackfriars Bridge, Ledger was photographed acting out a scene in which his character is apparently hanged by the neck in a noose under the bridge. After his death, disturbing photographs from the scene would appear on the Internet. Other snaps of Heath taken during his final year (including some taken during his London trip) show an unhealthy-looking man, seemingly older than his 28 years. Whether it was his dabbling in drugs, the increasing generalised anxiety and accompanying lack of sleep he was suffering from, career pressure or the split from Michelle Williams (or some combination of them all), the strain was showing on the young actor's once clean-cut and handsome face. He looked drawn and exhausted most of the time, and constant flying back and forth between New York and London during January 2008 was hardly conducive to good health or relaxation. Co-star Christopher Plummer had noticed Ledger's ill health during the London filming and feared he was suffering from 'walking pneumonia. We all caught colds, because we were shooting outside on horrible, damp nights,' said Plummer of their work in mid-January on the London location shoot. 'What's more, Heath was saying all the time, "Dammit, I can't sleep!" and he was taking all these pills.'

The London shoot for *The Imaginarium of Doctor Parnassus* wrapped on

Matilda's name written in cement outside the family house in Brooklyn.

Saturday, 19 January and Heath happily flew back to New York, hoping to spend some time with Matilda before reuniting with the film crew for further work, this time in Canada (where he shot *Brokeback Mountain*). However, spending time with his daughter was off the agenda, as Williams and Matilda were still in Sweden due to her commitments on *Mammoth*. This no doubt disappointed Heath – who hadn't seen Matilda for quite some time – and may have deepened his growing despondency.

Over his final weekend, Heath Ledger was seen buying coffee at Café Miro during the day on Sunday, one of his regular haunts. He wasn't inviting conversation, though, as he had his iPod earphones firmly attached. That night he was once again at the Beatrice Inn, but dressed in a truly bizarre fashion. Reports had the young actor wearing not only a hoodie, but also a ski mask, which effectively covered his face, making him look more like a burglar or a terrorist than a world-famous movie star. He spent the night drinking alone. Whether he was trying to avoid the paparazzi, or just hoping for some privacy in public, he can't have been anything but an unusual sight at the bar.

By Monday morning, the ski mask was gone, and Heath was in Le Pain Quotidien, close to his apartment, where he enjoyed a light meal, according to *People Magazine*'s account of his final days. Again, the actor was not inviting attention, as he had his iPod on full blast while eating a bowl of granola. According to one observer, 'He wasn't chatty – he looked like he wanted to be left alone.'

Heath attends the Rescue Dawn *premiere in support of his* I'm Not There *and* The Dark Knight *co-star Christian Bale.*

Early evening on Monday, Heath Ledger went grocery shopping at Gourmet Garage, again local to his apartment, where he was a regular shopper. Dropping in around 6pm, Ledger bought items that, according to the grocery-store clerk, suggested he was planning on preparing a meal. The actor left with three bags of groceries, including fruit and vegetables, alongside organic chicken sausages. Heath packed his bags himself and was described as 'very friendly, but pretty quiet'.

According to one uncorroborated account, Ledger spent Monday evening having dinner at East Village vegetarian restaurant Angelica Kitchen, with two unnamed women. Possibly the last person to speak with Ledger was his *The Four Feathers* director Shekhar Kapur. The pair had been discussing a variety of future projects, including one film in which Heath would play a television reporter whose station turns his war reports into a kind of reality-TV show. 'I last spoke to him the night before he died. I had just arrived in New York. He said he could not see me that night but really wanted to meet me the next day,' the 62-year-old Kapur said. 'He made me promise that I would call him in the morning and wake him up. I tried . . .'

Between Monday night and Tuesday morning, Heath Ledger was apparently alone. How did he spend his evening back at his spacious Broome Street apartment? Based on his recent track record, he probably had trouble sleeping. What was going through his mind? Among the things he had to think about would be worries concerning his current role in *The Imaginarium of Doctor Parnassus* – on *Brokeback Mountain* and *The Dark Knight*, Ledger had been unable to sleep due to his concerns about the work he was doing in front of the camera. Was he achieving all he wanted to with the character? Did he feel like a fraud once more, someone on the verge of being 'found out'?

'Last time I saw him he was lying face down. I didn't think anything was wrong; I thought he was sleeping.' – Teresa Solomon

As his anxiety increased, his loneliness overwhelmed him and, as the long, dark New York night wore on, Heath seems to have fallen back on his prescription medications to help him relax. He had several different types of pills, prescribed by doctors from different countries. Travelling due to his filming commitments meant he'd built up quite a supply of painkillers and sleeping pills. They'd worked in the past in allowing him to slip into oblivion and forget his cares for a few hours, but less so now. Heath probably remembered his attempts to sleep while making *The Dark Knight*, when he'd taken multiple Ambien to little positive effect. As the night passed into early morning, did Heath think he'd try a few more pills in order to allow him to rest, to give him a few hours of much sought-after sleep? Was he just tired, depressed, anxious and confused: did he forget how many pills he'd already taken and, half-awake, half-asleep, take some more? After all, they were prescribed by doctors, right: they must be safe. He wasn't taking hundreds, like suicides do, just a few in order to get some shut-eye. Intelligent though he was, Ledger doesn't seem to have considered the effect his multiple medications might have had in combination. Eventually, at some point during the long night, or early morning, he fell asleep. It was to be a final sleep from which he would not awake.

The morning of Tuesday, 22 January 2008 started just as any other for Heath Ledger's housekeeper, 56-year-old Teresa Solomon. Every Tuesday she'd visit Heath's apartment in order to clean up after the messy actor. Ledger had been living like any other single man, and he wasn't the neatest of people at the best of times. Solomon would let herself in with her key and set about cleaning the apartment, whether Ledger was in or not. She was even used to finding the actor sleeping in late after a night on the town.

'I last spoke to him the night before he died. I had just arrived in New York. He said he could not see me that night but really wanted to meet me the next day. He made me promise that I would call him in the morning and wake him up. I tried . . .'
– Shekhar Kapur

On this Tuesday, Solomon arrived at around 12:30pm and found a note stuck to the fridge door. Heath's handwritten scrawl warned her that he'd booked a masseuse to visit at 3pm. First item on the agenda for the housekeeper was to change a lightbulb in the bathroom next to Ledger's bedroom. According to CNN and Associated Press reports, Solomon claimed she saw the actor in bed and heard him snoring quietly. She had no reason to suspect there was anything untoward. 'Last time I saw him he was lying face down,' said Solomon. 'I didn't think anything was wrong; I thought he was sleeping.' The housekeeper returned to her duties, leaving the movie star to his privacy.

At 2:45pm, 40-year-old masseuse Diana Lee Wolozin arrived, slightly early for her 3pm appointment. An hour and 45 minutes had passed since Solomon had last seen Heath, but the two women spent the fifteen minutes up to around 3pm chatting, rather than rousing the apparently sleeping actor. By 3:10pm, Wolozin was concerned that her client had not awoken for his appointment, so she called him on his cell phone, hoping to rouse him from his sleep. She followed this by knocking loudly on his bedroom door. Again, there was no response from inside. Wolozin entered the bedroom, noting that Heath seemed to be still asleep. She began setting up her massage table, failing to realise there was anything wrong with the actor.

Ready to begin the delayed session, Wolozin attempted to physically rouse Ledger, but the actor's body was cold to the touch and he did not wake up. Finally realising that something was seriously wrong with her client, Wolozin decide to call for help. Rather than dial 911 for the emergency services, the befuddled masseuse called Heath's latest friend, 22-year-old Mary-Kate Olsen, using his own cell phone. She claimed she'd made that call, rather than one direct to 911, as she 'wanted to avoid a media circus'. She knew that Olsen was a friend of Heath's and felt she'd be the best one to call. However, Olsen was then in California, so there was little she could do herself, except send her own local security people to Heath's apartment.

Wolozin made two separate calls to Olsen between 3:17pm and 3:20pm, the second one being a more panicked call in which she expressed the fear that Heath might actually be dead and she was going to finally call 911, which she did at 3:26pm, but only after a third call to Olsen at 3:24pm. The 911 emergency operator instructed Wolozin on how to revive someone, while waiting for the paramedics to arrive.

Within seven minutes of being called, New York Fire Department paramedics were in the building at Broome Street, joined by Olsen's security team who arrived around the same time. The paramedics banned the security team from entering Heath's apartment while they went to work. They discovered the body of Heath Ledger, naked under a bed sheet. Nearby were several prescription pill bottles and a rolled-up $20 note. While the paramedics worked, Wolozin once again called Olsen at 3:34pm, keeping her up-to-date with developments. The paramedics moved Heath's body to the floor in their attempts to revive the actor. By the time the NYPD officers arrived minutes later, the paramedics had finished their work and Heath Ledger had been formally declared dead at 3:36pm.

'I'm not a resident of Australia. I've never voted in Australia. I'm a non-resident of America. I'm not really sure where I belong.' – Heath Ledger

As the police investigated the apartment, looking for any clues that might explain the death, they discovered six different types of medication, including two prescribed to treat anxiety, another two for insomnia and two more different types of painkillers. Three of the medications had been prescribed in Europe, and it was unlikely that any of the doctors involved had been able to compare notes about the medications that Ledger was apparently taking. No illegal drugs were found in the apartment and there was no evidence that Ledger had been consuming alcohol. Initially, partly due to the rolled $20 note (often used to snort cocaine), the police looked upon the death as a possible suicide (even though there was no sign of a suicide note) or even a drug overdose, but they knew they'd have to wait for a full autopsy before a proper cause of death could be determined.

Across the world, in Perth, Australia, Ledger's family were to discover the news of his unexpected death from the media. According to Heath's uncle, his mother's brother Neil Bell, 'His mother and father heard of his death on the news. We are all devastated. The whole family is devastated over his death, and more so over having to learn [it] from the media.'

As Heath's body was being removed from the Broome Street apartment at 6:28pm, news of the actor's death had spread far and wide. Thanks to the worldwide reach of the Internet and the hungry needs of the 24/7 news cycle, the brief police statement issued about the actor's demise had reached almost every corner of the world. TV crews were waiting to film the body being removed, and a crowd of about 800 people stood outside in the cold, many with camera phones, striving to capture the moment.

Ledger's family issued a statement confirming their son's shocking death, but affirming that, if a drug overdose was responsible, it was almost certainly accidental rather than intentional suicide. The statement was read out in front of waiting TV cameras by Heath's father Kim, flanked by the actor's mother, Sally, and sister, Kate. 'Heath's family confirms the very tragic, untimely and accidental passing of our dearly loved son, brother and doting father of Matilda. He was found peacefully asleep in his New York apartment by his housekeeper at 3:30pm US time. We would like to thank our friends and everyone around the world for their well wishes and kind thoughts at this time. Heath has touched so many people on so many different levels during his short life but few had the pleasure of truly knowing him. He was a down-to-earth, generous, kind-hearted, life-loving and selfless individual who was extremely inspirational to many. Please now respect our family's need to grieve and come to terms with our loss privately.'

It wasn't long before many of those who knew or worked with Heath Ledger responded to the news of the actor's passing. Helena Christensen was one of the first, as she had been due to hook up with Heath on the day he died. 'I was on my way over to pay him a visit when I found out,' she said. 'I had just left him a message and heard his voice on the [answering] machine.'

After hearing the unbelievable news late in her hotel on Tuesday evening in Trollhattan, Sweden, where she was still filming *Mammoth*, Michelle Williams quickly made arrangements for her and Matilda to return to the US, with the pair arriving back in Brooklyn on Wednesday evening. Initially Williams ignored the media, making no comment, but her father Larry did speak. 'It has just broken everybody's heart in my family. My heart goes out to everyone, his family, my family, we are just very saddened. The saddest thing is his daughter, whom he just loved dearly.'

'Working with Heath was one of the purest joys of my life. His death is heartbreaking.' – Ang Lee

Days later, Michelle finally broke her silence, saying, 'I am the mother of the most tender-hearted, high-spirited, beautiful little girl who is the spitting image of her father. All that I can cling to is his presence inside her that reveals itself every day,' before adding, 'Please respect our need to grieve privately.' Of their shared daughter, Michelle said, 'His family and I watch Matilda as she whispers to trees, hugs animals, and takes steps two at a time, and we know that he is with us still. She will be brought up in the best memories of him.'

Reaction across the world was swift, with an outpouring of grief and shock, mainly due to Ledger's young age and now-to-be unrealised potential. For an actor of such promise to have his career and life with his young family cut short in such a manner was disturbing to many. As the flowers left by fans and admirers began to pile up outside Ledger's Broome Street apartment, back in Perth the family were beginning to think about flying to the US in order to make the necessary funeral arrangements. Heath's father, Kim, became the de facto family spokesman, and he was determined to discover the true cause of his son's death as media speculation about his supposed hard-partying, drug-taking ways intensified.

Days after the actor's death, video footage of him taken at an Oscars party in the Chateau Marmont hotel in Hollywood emerged in which he seemingly admitted to regular drug use. As other partygoers were seen to snort from a table described as being 'filled with drugs', Ledger was heard to say, in a slurred voice, 'I used to smoke five joints a day for 20 years,' something probably impossible for a mere 28-year-old. He continued, 'I'm gonna get so much shit from my girlfriend. We had a baby three months ago. I shouldn't be here at all.' The footage was aired on American TV on *Entertainment Tonight* and fuelled speculation that the actor had accidentally overdosed on illegal drugs. Later, a lawsuit would allege that Heath had been deliberately framed by two members of the paparazzi, who were determined to capture footage of him doing drugs, even if they had to set him up.

Actors and directors who'd worked with Heath were swift to pay tribute as they heard the news of his death. 'He was just taking off and to lose his life at such a young age is a tragic loss,' said his *The Patriot* co-star and mentor Mel Gibson. Fellow Australian Nicole Kidman called Heath's death a 'terrible tragedy'. His *I'm Not There* co-star Cate Blanchett said, 'I deeply respected Heath's work and always admired his continuing development as an artist,' and continued that she was 'shocked and very saddened by the news. My thoughts are with his family and close friends.'

'Working with Heath was one of the purest joys of my life,' said *Brokeback Mountain* director Ang Lee. 'He brought to the role of Ennis more than any of us could have imagined – a thirst for life, for love, and for truth, and a vulnerability that made everyone who knew him love him. His death is heartbreaking.'

'Charisma – as invisible and natural as gravity. That's what Heath had.' – Christopher Nolan

Neil Armfield, who'd directed Ledger in drug addiction drama *Candy*, noted, 'He made a decision about four years ago to stop being led by producers and managers and to forge his own way. He started working with the most interesting directors. He was so successful at breaking out of the teen idol image.'

Through his producers on *The Imaginarium of Doctor Parnassus*, Terry Gilliam paid tribute to Ledger as 'a great actor, a great friend and a great spirit. We are still in a state of deep shock, saddened and numb with grief.' Mary-Kate Olsen, the first person called to be told of Heath's death, said, 'Heath was a friend. His death is a tragic loss. My thoughts are with his family during this very difficult time.'

John Travolta, who hadn't worked with Heath but was in Australia at the time of the actor's death, said he'd been one of his favourite performers. 'I adored him. I don't know how to compare his talent to others but he's touched me deeply as a talent and it's a great loss – losing him at any age would be a loss but it was pretty rough news. I was really shocked by it,' he said. Even recently elected Australian Prime Minister Kevin Rudd paid tribute, calling the star 'one of our nation's finest actors'.

Headmaster Robert Zordan, still running Heath's old school Guildford Grammar, recalled his pupil's 'passion for drama. His public life meant people at Guildford Grammar followed his successes. One of the great things was that with all the stardom there was a degree of humility.'

A face in the crowd. Heath walks alone through Chinatown, New York, in October 2007, three months before his death.

Even the White House reacted, postponing an event planned for the day after Heath died to promote an advertising campaign aimed at preventing prescription-drug abuse. 'We thought it would be better to postpone the event rather than run the risk of anyone thinking that we were being opportunistic in highlighting the issue,' said White House press secretary Dana Perino.

Although the initial autopsy on Heath Ledger was inconclusive as to cause of death, test results which came back ten days later were clear. The toxicology results confirmed the actor had suffered 'acute intoxication' but not an overdose, caused by mixing prescription medicines, just what the White House's advertising campaign launch was to warn against. The result said his death was caused by 'the combined effects of oxycodone, hydrocodone, diazepam, temazepam, alprazolam and doxylamine' in his system.

'His acting was so touching, so connected in truth. I think he was just getting started.' – Naomi Watts

The results pointed to death by a combination of drugs that alone and in moderation would not otherwise have been fatal. Oxycodone and hydrocodone were pain relievers derived from codeine, the latter the main ingredient in Vicodin. Three of the drugs were ingredients of commonly available (in the US) anti-anxiety medicines: alprazolam (Xanax), diazepam (Valium) and temazepam (Restoril, a sleep medication). The final drug, doxylamine, was an ingredient in widely available sleep aids and cold remedies. The medical examiner's spokesperson Ellen Borakove concluded that 'the manner of death is accidental, resulting from the abuse of prescription medicines'. The individual medicines on their own were fine, but in combination they proved fatal. 'It's the combination of drugs that caused the problem,' said Borakove, 'not necessarily too much of any particular drug. All these drugs have a cumulative effect on the body.'

The US Federal Drug Enforcement Administration (DEA) took an interest in the Ledger case, determined to track down the source of the medicines, as they are legally required to do in a death where illegal drugs may have been involved. Having investigated the circumstances and the doctors in California and Texas, the DEA cleared those involved. After all, if patients go to multiple doctors and perhaps lie about the drugs they're already taking, it can't be the doctor's responsibility for the patient's subsequent conduct.

Kim Ledger responded to the toxicology findings, saying, 'We remain humble as parents and a family, among millions of people worldwide who may have suffered the tragic loss of a child. Few can understand the hollow, wrenching and enduring agony parents silently suffer when a child predeceases them. Today's results put an end to speculation, but our son's beautiful spirit and enduring memory will forever remain in our hearts.'

He went on to address the medical examiner's findings directly. 'While no medications were taken in excess, we learned today the combination of doctor-prescribed drugs proved lethal for our boy. Heath's accidental death serves as a caution to the hidden dangers of combining prescription medication, even at low dosage.'

Heath's father then fondly recalled the two weeks the entire family had spent together over Christmas 2007, immediately before the actor's return to New York and his untimely death. 'Our family enjoyed an extremely happy two-week visit with Heath just prior to the New Year. Those recent precious days will stay with us forever. We as a family feel privileged to have some of his amazing magic moments captured in film. To most of the world Heath was an actor of immeasurable talent and promise. To those who knew him personally, Heath was a consummate artist whose passions also included photography, music, chess and directing. We knew Heath as a loving father, as our devoted son, and as a loyal and generous brother and friend.'

Finally, Kim Ledger talked of his granddaughter and pleaded for the world's media to leave the family in peace. 'We treasure our beautiful granddaughter Matilda (to our dear Michelle) as well as an unbelievably wonderful network of close friends, forever, around the world. Families rarely experience the uplifting, warm and massive outpouring of grief and support as have we, from every corner of the planet. This has deeply and profoundly touched our hearts and lives. We are eternally grateful. At this moment we respectfully request the worldwide media allow us time to grieve privately, without the intrusions associated with press and photography.'

'I just feel so sad about what we're being deprived of and the work that he would have continued to bring to us. He just seemed like he was on a different plane.'
– Todd Haynes

Heath Ledger's body was released to the family and held at the Frank E. Campbell funeral chapel on Madison Avenue in New York. Having been in business since 1898, the establishment had handled its fair share of famous clients, from silent-movie star Rudolph Valentino (who died young) to assassinated Beatle John Lennon, *The Wizard of Oz* star Judy Garland and movie gangster James Cagney. On 25 January, the family had the body transferred to Los Angeles, en route to Heath's final resting place in Perth, Australia. Saturday night saw a private memorial event held at the Perth funeral home, for close family and friends only, including Michelle Williams, Naomi Watts and Heath's *Candy* co-star Abbie Cornish. Kim Ledger returned to New York the following Wednesday to clear out Heath's Broome Street apartment (which was soon re-rented, at an even higher rate than before), then flew on to Los Angeles to attend a 90-minute remembrance service held on the Sony studio lot at Culver City. In attendance were many who'd worked with Ledger and many more who simply admired the actor and his sadly now complete body of work. Tom Cruise and his wife Katie Holmes were there, alongside Ellen DeGeneres, Naomi Watts, Shannyn Sossamon, Gemma Ward, Lindsay Lohan, Orlando Bloom and Sienna Miller. Michelle Williams and Matilda were not in attendance.

Saturday, 9 February saw the Ledgers, Michelle and Matilda, along with many more of Heath's Australian friends and colleagues, assemble for a final memorial service in Perth. Cate Blanchett was a speaker at the service, along with *Candy* director Neil Armfield, *Two Hands* co-star Bryan Brown and *Ned Kelly* actor Joel

Flowers and candles left outside 421 Broome Street, the SoHo apartment where Heath's body was discovered.

Edgerton. Heath's life was celebrated through remembrances, film clips and songs. Ben Harper's 'Happy Ever After', written for Matilda, was played live and local musician Levi Islam played on the traditional Aboriginal didgeridoo, an instrument Ledger had once tried to learn. Kim Ledger told reporters, 'We're finding it pretty difficult to cope by ourselves, let alone with everyone else around the world. Having said that, we do really appreciate the outpouring and the emotional support from all over the globe.'

Although 500 people attended the memorial service at Penrhos College, in the Perth suburb of Como, a very private funeral followed for immediate family members only at Fremantle Cemetery. Heath Ledger's body was cremated, as Michelle Williams read Shakespeare's *Sonnet 18*, which begins 'Shall I compare thee to a summer's day?'

A more celebratory wake followed at the Indiana Tea House on Cottesloe Beach – one of Heath's favourite places in Perth. Williams, clearly upset by the private funeral service, attended wearing dark glasses to conceal her tears. As the afternoon sun waned, some of the mourners spontaneously took to the sea, dancing at the water's edge, including a visibly recovered Michelle. The location was Heath's favourite spot for surfing when he was growing up, and every trip back to Australia he'd try to catch a few waves here. It seemed like a fitting end to the day's celebrations of the tragic actor's life.

The aftermath of Heath Ledger's death was a confusing time for many, including his family and fans worldwide. He left behind two unreleased films. The Batman sequel, *The Dark Knight*, had been virtually completed and Heath had wrapped his role as the Joker. Director Chris Nolan recalled Ledger's 'charisma – as invisible and natural as gravity' – in a piece for *Newsweek* magazine. 'One time he and another actor were shooting a complex scene. We had two days to shoot it, and at the end of the first day, they'd really found something and Heath was worried that he might not have it if we stopped. He wanted to carry on and finish. It's tough to ask the crew to work late when we all know there's plenty of time to finish the next day. But everyone seemed to understand that Heath had something special and that we had to capture it before it disappeared. Months later, I learned that, as Heath left the set that night, he quietly thanked each crewmember for working late. Quietly. Not trying to make a point, just grateful for the chance to create that they'd given him.'

Further tributes to Heath decorate the SoHo sidewalk.

As *The Dark Knight* was being prepared for release, test audiences reacted to two scenes featuring Ledger that Warner Bros. and Nolan considered cutting. One scene featured Heath's Joker 'playing dead' by hiding in a body bag. Test-screening audiences reacted in a very uncomfortable way, 'gasping, shuffling and murmuring', with an overall atmosphere of unease, according to someone in attendance. Obviously, the scene took on a whole new meaning in the wake of Ledger's death. The second scene saw Ledger riffing on one of the most famous lines from *Brokeback Mountain*, 'I wish I knew how to quit you,' as delivered to Ennis by Jake Gyllenhaal's Jack. In *The Dark Knight*, the Joker says a similar line sarcastically to Christian Bale's Batman. Both scenes were reconsidered by Warner Bros. and director Christopher Nolan, but were due to be left intact for the film's July release in the US.

'As we started my cut, I would wonder about each take we chose, each trim we made,' Nolan said of the editing process. 'I would visualise the screening where we'd have to show Heath the finished film – sitting three or four rows behind him, watching the movements of his head for clues to what he was thinking about what we'd done with all that he'd given us. Now that screening will never be real.'

Heath's last film was still in production when he died. Terry Gilliam came up with a novel way to complete *The Imaginarium of Doctor Parnassus*, while also allowing some of Ledger's contemporaries and admirers to pay tribute to him through their performances. Johnny Depp, Colin Farrell and Jude Law would all play aspects of Ledger's character Toby, as he is magically transformed through the film. This would not only allow Gilliam to complete the movie, but it also gave the whole project a unique, positive selling point. Shooting had been halted following Ledger's death, but resumed in Vancouver in March 2008, with the movie scheduled for release in 2009.

Beyond the remaining movies, Ledger's passing had a more immediate impact on his family. Once past the immediate shock and grief, and the process of the funerals and tributes, things settled down for the Ledgers, until the unveiling of Heath's will. The *New York Daily News* reported that the most up-to-date will for Heath Ledger dated from 2003 and so made no provision for Michelle Williams or his two-year-old daughter Matilda. Heath left everything to his sister and parents, according to documents filed in a Manhattan court, which also showed that the movie star had less than $145,000 in assets at the time of his death. The papers revealed that Ledger's family spent more than $39,000 on a memorial service for Ledger at Frank E. Campbell Funeral Home, including $25,000 for his casket and $450 for 40 certified copies of his death certificate. Ledger's only assets apparently included a car worth $25,000 and $20,000 in furniture and fixtures, as well as $100,000 spread across various bank accounts. Not a lot to show for a movie career that saw some roles pay him fees in the millions of dollars range. Where had Heath's money gone?

'I think that the interesting thing about Heath, which maybe people have only really fully discovered in his death, is how vulnerable he was. You can pick up on it in his performances, but it's easy to overlook because he was so physical and beautiful and strong and masculine. But there was always that underlying sensitivity. That's who he was.' – Michelle Williams

Ledger's father Kim maintained that Michelle and Matilda 'would be taken care of', but he provided no details. 'Matilda is our absolute priority and Michelle is an integral part of our family. They will be taken care of and that's how Heath would want it to be.'

This was not enough for Williams's father Larry, who felt that Ledger's true assets were being hidden. 'It's real simple: just come clean with everything,' he said, in a message aimed at Heath's father. 'It's so easy to resolve this [doubt]. He [Kim Ledger] just has to say where the income went and where the assets are. I'm certain that there is grieving in the Ledger family but [lawyers for] Kim have already filed papers in New York, so it seems like it's time to be transparent about it. I have no idea what Heath Ledger was worth [but] they certainly haven't stated all of the assets to the court.'

Larry Williams wasn't alone in raising questions about Kim Ledger's handling of Heath's estate. His brother, Mike Ledger, Heath's uncle and godfather, also spoke out. He maintained that Kim had a bad track record of estate management, and had mismanaged the estate of their grandfather Sir Frank Ledger fifteen years previously. 'It plunged into enormous debt,' claimed Mike Ledger. 'Our only vested interest is to assure that Matilda is well looked after. When you are talking about large sums of money like this it should be an independent executor, but Kim hasn't chosen [to do it] that way.' He went on to claim that, as the brothers had been feuding ever since their grandfather died, seventeen family members weren't invited to attend Heath's memorial

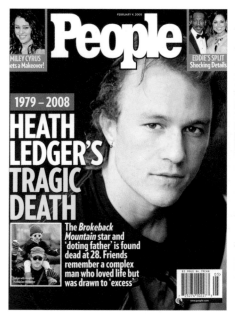
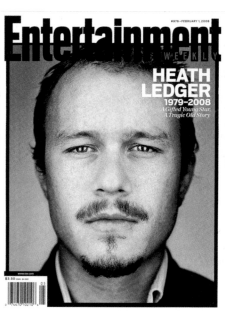

Heath Ledger's death shocked the world and instigated a global media frenzy.

'In *Brokeback Mountain* he was unique. He was perfect. And that scene in the trailer at the end of the film is as moving as anything I have ever seen.' – Daniel Day-Lewis

and funeral in Perth. 'I'm his godfather,' Mike said. 'I didn't even have the opportunity to pay my last respects to Heath. And I tell you, that is terrible – that is so sad.' An Australian executor of Heath's will who had known the Ledger family for 30 years, Robert John Collins, claimed that Mike's allegations about Kim were 'rubbish'.

Things took a further turn for the bizarre when another of Heath's uncles claimed the actor might have fathered a 'love child' while just seventeen. Haydn Ledger told Sydney's *Daily Telegraph* newspaper that 'There is a very real possibility that Heath was the father' of a child that resulted when young Heath developed a relationship with a 25-year-old woman. The unnamed woman allegedly found out she was pregnant with a baby girl after their relationship had ended and she was living with another man. 'She had the baby. Everyone lived under the assumption that she was the daughter of the mother's boyfriend and that is how she has been brought up,' an anonymous 'family member' was reported as having said. Naturally, the bizarre story was denied by the Ledgers and by the woman concerned, who maintained her anonymity and that of her now eleven-year-old daughter. The woman's husband, stepfather to the daughter, said, 'The whole thing with Ledger being the father is not true. No way. No can be. We knew it would flare up and that is the point of my talking and the simple thing is we will do a DNA test. I'm the stepdad, but there's nothing to hide and if I asked the

Heath Ledger in Brokeback Mountain. He lacked a Hollywood survival strategy

LONESOME COWBOY

1979–2008
HEATH LEDGER

The last interview
By Sarah Lyall

Heath Ledger in 2006.
Photograph by
Bryce Duffy/Corbis

HEATH LEDGER
1979 – 2008

Fallen Star

With his fearless role in the Oscar-winning 'Brokeback Mountain,' the Aussie actor became far more than just a pretty face. Now with his untimely death, a career—and a life—ends too soon.

BY JOSH ROTTENBERG

broken star

Drug abuse, depression and a lost love — the truth about the lonely death of the star of Brokeback Mountain

Cinema icon: Above, in Brokeback Mountain. Left, Lily Cole, filming in London the now-abandoned The Imaginarium of Dr Parnassus

HEATH LEDGER
1979 - 2008

A LIFE CUT SHORT

He had a red-hot career and a daughter he adored. But at 28, the actor was found dead in his New York apartment. How the life of one of Hollywood's brightest young stars came apart

TOO LATE TO SAVE HIM

We only had a glimpse of what might have been...

Ledger's death robs us of a tantalising talent whose gifts were often unworthy of his gifts, says Sheila Johnston

People

HEATH LEDGER

DID HE HAVE A SECRET CHILD?

Shocking reports rock the late star's family

HEATH LEDGER

SUDDEN DEATH IN JANUARY MADE HEADLINES, BUT THE PEOPLE CLOSEST TO THE ACTOR HAVE REMAINED QUIET. HERE, THEY OPEN UP FOR THE FIRST TIME ABOUT THE MAN THEY KNEW, LOVED, AND LOST

screen
Go gently, good knight

JAMES CHRISTOPHER pays tribute to Heath Ledger and the roles that might have been

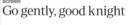

He was, if not at the

Issue 678
February 11, 2008

WEEKLY

Us

Heath Ledger's Secret Struggles

- A gifted actor's pain & battles with addiction
- Michelle Williams' lonely fight to save her soulmate

HEATH LEDGER

Forever young: Hollywood's fallen stars

death of Heath Ledger at the of 28 shows what fame can do young actor: David Gritten at the extraordinary pressures success in the movies brings

EATH OF A TORMENTED IDOL

from Peter Sheridan in Las Vegas

Heath Ledger was the film heart-throb for a new generation. But just before he died at 28 he revealed how turmoil in his personal life and the pressures of Hollywood were taking a terrible toll on him

"Oh, I definitely feared it. Although anything that makes me afraid I guess excites me at the same time. I certainly had to put on a brave face and believe that I had something up my sleeve. Something different."

Friends and family turn mourning into celebration by swimming in the ocean at sunset during Heath's wake in Perth.

mother I'm sure that she wouldn't mind having a DNA test.'

The woman herself added, 'I'm not answering anything. I think it's very, very rude that I'm being posed all of this. I really do. I can't talk about anything. There's no background, there's no grounds, there's no nothing.'

Heath's other uncle, Mike, called the allegation 'absolutely berserk', claiming the whole situation was a misunderstanding. 'All my brother Haydn said was that anything is possible,' claimed Mike, trying to put the story to bed. 'Haydn was asked a question that wasn't directly related to the Heath issue: "If someone was this age, could it be possible?" and Haydn said, "Anything is possible," and that's it. His statement was absolutely taken out of context. Absolutely. At the end of the day, our thoughts are with the little girl in question, and we're not prepared to make any more comments at all.'

Heath Ledger's 29th birthday would have been on 4 April 2008, and the date was marked by further tributes from friends and family. However, even four months after Heath's untimely passing there seemed to be no end to the new stories that surfaced about him. As the movie-hype machine began to build up to the July release of *The Dark Knight*, Joker-mania developed, and an action figure of Ledger's character was released.

A lawsuit filed on Friday, 11 April revealed the alleged truth behind the controversial party video of Heath talking about his drug consumption. The suit, against Hollywood photo agency Splash News & Picture Agency, claimed two of its paparazzi supplied the actor with cocaine so they could secretly videotape him snorting the drug in a hotel room two years before his death. The suit claimed that the footage of the Ledger encounter, a portion of which aired briefly on two US television shows days after his death in January, was sold to media outlets around the world, including in Britain and his native Australia. A former freelancer for *People* magazine, named only as Jane Doe, was also the former girlfriend of one of the paparazzi concerned and had brought the suit. Her attorney, Douglas Johnson, described her as 'a kind of whistle-blower. This is bad stuff. You don't give drug addicts drugs so you can tape them.' It seemed confirmation that Ledger's seeming paranoia about the activities of the paparazzi may not have been misplaced after all.

Michelle Williams is comforted at Heath's wake. Earlier that day she had read Shakespeare's Sonnet 18 *as his body was cremated.*

Heath Ledger was a movie star who burned brightly for the brief period he was famous. His career spanned just a decade, from 1999's *10 Things I Hate About You* to 2009's *The Imaginarium of Doctor Parnassus*. Although he seems to have spent much of his career on horseback, he played diverse characters in a wide range of movies; from a teen comedy (*10 Things . . .*) to period action adventure (*A Knight's Tale*), from historical epics (*The Patriot, The Four Feathers, Ned Kelly, Casanova*) to magical fantasies (*The Order, The Brothers Grimm, The Dark Knight, The Imaginarium of Doctor Parnassus*), Ledger tackled them all. He generally stayed away from contemporary-set dramas, with only *Monster's Ball* and *Lords of Dogtown* falling into that category (and even *Dogtown* was set in the 1970s). He even tried an 'art movie' with *I'm Not There*.

'Forget about his death and remember what's left to a lot of people in Australia, and – I guess – the world. And that is: if you've got a dream, follow it, do it.'
– Haydn Ledger, Heath's uncle

The one film he will be remembered for above all others is *Brokeback Mountain*. His Oscar-nominated performance showed he was an actor full of potential, and those who worked with him or even just saw his work expected great things in the future. His tentative thoughts about moving into directing showed that Heath was not going to be content with playing characters and following others' directions forever: he wanted to be a creative force in his own right.

His life off-screen was a full one, with many true, loyal friends and colleagues. His major relationships with Christina Cauchi, Heather Graham, Naomi Watts and Michelle Williams came to define him, especially that with Williams. The arrival of his daughter Matilda Rose gave Heath a new focus in life, away from movies and all the aggravations that came with being famous.

It's all the more tragic, then, that those elements of his personality that gave the world great performances like those in *Brokeback Mountain* and *The Dark Knight* were the same things that resulted in his suffering great anxiety and uncertainty about his own abilities and talents. His Oscar nomination for *Brokeback Mountain* seemed to worry Ledger rather than spur him on to new achievements. He now had a standard to live up to, a challenge he thought would be difficult.

'I'm still a kid. I'm like six-years-old. It's just a big journey. I felt like when I left home that I was on a journey, and I still am.' – Heath Ledger

Harassed by the paparazzi, suffering from anxiousness and insomnia, the final straw may have been the split from Michelle Williams and the damage it was doing to his relationship with his daughter, Matilda. These events may have been enough to send the already fragile actor into a spiral of depression and anguish that could have led to him, wittingly or unwittingly, abusing drugs both illegal and prescribed. Heath Ledger didn't want to die at the age of 28: he had too much to live for, both professionally and personally. But he was a fragile personality, one that needed looking out for. At the start of 2008, no one was looking out for Heath Ledger, and the despairing actor made a terrible mistake.

His sixteen films will go on entertaining his fans, and into the future new fans will discover the work of Heath Ledger. They will wonder, with us, about what might have been if he'd been able to overcome his demons and deliver the fantastic screen career and life that all who knew him thought he was capable of. His unexpected and tragic death has made such an impact it seems unlikely that movie audiences will be able to quit Heath Ledger any time soon.

'Heath was so particular and so individual,' said Amy Pascal. 'It's like losing a star, a light.'

British Library Cataloguing in Publication Data
    Robb, Brian J.
    Heath Ledger : Hollywood's dark star
    1. Ledger, Heath, 1979-2008 2. Motion picture actors and
    actresses – Australia – Biography
    I. Title
    791.4'3'028'092

ISBN-10: 0-85965-427-3
ISBN-13: 978-0-85965-427-2

Cover photograph by Nicolas Guerin/Corbis Limited
Printed in Spain by Vivapress
Book and cover design by Coco Wake-Porter

ACKNOWLEDGEMENTS

A book such as this cannot be completed – especially on time
– without the help, patience and perseverance of a lot of
people. Thanks to our editorial team – Tom Branton and
Paul Woods – who stepped in with additional research and
writing when the author was taken ill. Without their
unflagging effort and meticulous attention to detail many
loose ends would have remained untied. Thanks also to
Harvey Weinig and Alice Moray for their speedy and sterling
work, researching material from the United States. Special
thanks to Coco Wake-Porter for her patience and creativity
in designing this book.
    Heath Ledger gave interviews to many newspapers and
magazines over the years, and these have proved invaluable in
chronicling his life and his attitude to his work. The author
would like to give special thanks to the Sydney Daily
Telegraph and People Magazine, as well as the following:
Vanity Fair; West Magazine; the New York Daily News;
Access Hollywood; Variety; Entertainment Weekly; the New
York Times; Film Australia; the Herald Sun; the Chicago Sun
Times; the San Francisco Chronicle; Film Threat; the Toronto
Globe and Mail; the New York Post; Atlanta Journal-
Constitution; the Los Angeles Times; the Los Angeles Daily
News; the Guardian; the Hollywood Reporter; Premiere
Magazine; Empire Magazine; Boston Globe; the Wall Street
Journal; Wonderland Magazine; the Sunday Times; the
Observer; Independent on Sunday; Mail on Sunday; the
Times; US Weekly; Interview Magazine; Entertainment; the
Perth Sunday Times; Melbourne Herald Sun; the Age; West
Australian; Teen People Magazine; the Village Voice; Rolling
Stone; the Sydney Morning Herald.
    Thanks are also due to the film distributors for Heath
Ledger's movies. Film stills courtesy of: CML Films; Meridian
Films; Beyond Films International; Buena Vista Home
Entertainment; Future Film; Miramax Home Entertainment;
Barron Entertainment; 7 Network; Touchstone Pictures; Mad
Chance; Jaret Entertainment; Buena Vista Pictures; Sea
Change Productions; Universal TV; Fox Network; Studios
USA Television; Colombia Pictures Corporation; Centropolis
Entertainment; Mutual Film Company; Global Entertainment
Productions GmbH; Black and Blu Entertainment; Columbia
Pictures Corporation; Escape Artists; Finestkind; Lee Daniels
Entertainment; Lions Gate Films; Belhaven Limited; Dune
Films; Jaffilms; Marty Katz Productions; The Australian Film
Commission; Australian Film Finance Corporation; Studio
Canal; Working Title Films; Twentieth Century Fox Film
Corporation; Colombia Pictures Corporation; Mosaic Media
Group; Metro-Goldwyn-Mayer; The Weinstein Company;
Alberta Films; Paramount Pictures; Touchstone Pictures; Film
Finance; Killer Films; Warner Bros. Pictures; Davis-Films;
Grosvenor Park Productions; Infinity Features Entertainments.
    We would like to thank the many Heath Ledger fan
websites, works of devotion that were extremely helpful as
referenced sources: Heathbaby.com; Heathledger.net; My
space.com/heathaledger; Heathledger.com; Heathheathens.net
as well as the web sites imdb.com; cnn.com; bbc.co.uk.
    We would like to thank the following for supplying
photographs: Getty Images/Fox p.32; Getty
Images/WireImage/Bob Riha Jr. p.38; Getty Images/Wire
Image/Beyond Films/Meridian Films/The Kobal
Collection/Kobal p.41; Getty Images/FilmMagic/Jeff Kravitz
p.73; Getty Images/WireImage/S Granitz p.96; Getty
Images/Photonews International Inc.p.133; Getty
Images/Photonews International Inc. p.135; Getty
Images/WireImage/Theo Wargo p.138; Getty
Images/FilmMagic/Jon Kopaloff p.139; Getty Images/Gareth
Cattermole p.141; Getty Images/Patrick Riviere p.145;
Getty Images/Lucky Mat p.146; Getty Images/Lucky Mat
p.161; Getty Images/Frazer Harrison p.148; Getty
Images/Vera Anderson p.150; Getty Images/WireImage/Jesse
Grant p.162; Getty Image/WireImage/Djamilla Cochran
p.181; Getty Images/Brad Barket p.188; Getty
Images/WireImage/Jean Baptiste Lacroix p.195; Getty
Images/WireImage/Jason Kempin p.198; Getty
Images/WireImage/James Devaney p.199; Getty
Images/Matt Jelonek p.204; Getty Images/Matt Jelonek
p.205; Getty Images/Carlo Allegri p.172; Getty
Images/Carlo Allegri p.206; Corbis Outline/Ben Watts p.2;
Corbis Outline/Ben Watts p.4; Corbis Outline/Stephen
Oxenbury p.6; Corbis/Sygma/Marcel Hartmann p.12;
Corbis/Bryce Duffy p.98; Bigpicturesphoto.com p.116;
Bigpicturesphoto.com p.165; Bigpicturesphoto.com/Paul
Chesterton/Craig Ross p.167; Bigpicturesphoto.com/GIG
p.170; Bigpicturesphoto.com p.176; Bigpicturesphoto.com
p.177; Bigpicturesphoto.com/ Eagle Eyes/Leon McGowran
p.185; AAP Image/Kylee Young p.36; AAP Image/REP
Films p.42; AAP Image p.43; AAP Image p.48; AAP Image
p.53; Rex Features/ Newspix p.11; Rex Features/Newspix
p.14; Rex Features/Newspix p.17; Rex Features/Newspix
p.18; Rex Features/Newspix p.27; Rex Features/Newspix
p.30; Rex Features/Newspix p.45; Rex Features/Alecsey
Boldeskul p.143; Rex Features/Dave Allocca p.189; Rex
Features/Steve Connolly p.158; Moviestore Collection.
    The author would like to thank Dr Mistry and the Acute
Assessment Unit Staff at West Middlesex Hospital for their
time and attention during his unexpected bout with
pneumonia, and to everyone at Titan, especially Jonathan
Wilkins, for stepping in during his enforced absence.
    Every effort has been made to acknowledge and trace
copyright holders and to contact original sources, and we
apologise for any unintentional errors which will be corrected
in any future editions of this book.